C000175773

The
HIDDEN PLACES
of
NORTH WALES

including
Snowdonia & Isle of Anglesey

Edited by
Joanna Billing

© Travel Publishing Ltd. 1998

Published by:
Travel Publishing Ltd
7a Apollo House, Calleva Park
Aldermaston, Berks, RG7 8TN

ISBN 1-902-00718-2

© Travel Publishing Ltd 1998

First Published:	*1989*
Second Edition:	*1993*
Third Edition:	*1998*

Regional Titles in the Hidden Places Series:

Cambridgeshire & Lincolnshire	Channel Islands
Cheshire	Cornwall
Devon	Dorset, Hants & Isle of Wight
Essex	Gloucestershire
Heart of England	Highlands & Islands
Kent	Lake District & Cumbria
Lancashire	Norfolk
Northeast Yorkshire	Northumberland & Durham
North Wales	Nottinghamshire
Peak District	Potteries
Somerset	South Wales
Suffolk	Surrey
Sussex	Thames & Chilterns
Warwickshire & W Midlands	Welsh Borders
Wiltshire	Yorkshire Dales

National Titles in the Hidden Places Series:

England	Ireland
Scotland	Wales

Printing by: Nuffield Press, Abingdon
Maps by: © MAPS IN MINUTES ™ (1998)
Line Drawings: Sarah Bird
Editor: Joanna Billing
Cover : Clare Hackney

Born in 1961, Clare was educated at West Surrey College of Art and Design as well as studying at Kingston University. She runs her own private water-colour school based in Surrey and has exhibited both in the UK and internationally. The cover is taken from an original water-colour of the Pontcysyllte Aqueduct at Cefn-mawr.

All information is included by the publishers in good faith and is believed to be correct at the time of going to press. No responsibility can be accepted for errors.

This book is sold subject to the condition that it shall not by way of trade or otherwise be lent, re-sold, hired out, or otherwise circulated without the publisher's prior consent in any form of binding or cover other than that which it is published and without similar condition including this condition being imposed on the subsequent purchase.

FOREWORD

The Hidden Places series is a collection of easy to use travel guides taking you, in this instance, on a relaxed but informative tour through North Wales, a region which is rich in history and heritage but which is also blessed with a very varied landscape of mountains, vales, forests,heaths, moorlands and a spectacular coastline. Our books contain a wealth of interesting information on the history, the countryside, the towns and villages and the more established places of interest in the county. But they also promote the more secluded and little known visitor attractions and places to stay, eat and drink many of which are easy to miss unless you know exactly where you are going.

We include hotels, inns, restaurants, public houses, teashops, various types of accommodation, historic houses, museums, gardens, garden centres, craft centres and many other attractions throughout North Wales, all of which are comprehensively indexed. Most places have an attractive line drawing and are cross-referenced to coloured maps found at the rear of the book. We do not award merit marks or rankings but concentrate on describing the more interesting, unusual or unique features of each place with the aim of making the reader's stay in the local area an enjoyable and stimulating experience.

Whether you are visiting the area for business or pleasure or in fact are living in the county we do hope that you enjoy reading and using this book. We are always interested in what readers think of places covered (or not covered) in our guides so please do not hesitate to use the reader reaction forms provided to give us your considered comments. We also welcome any general comments which will help us improve the guides themselves. Finally if you are planning to visit any other corner of the British Isles we would like to refer you to the list of other *Hidden Places* titles to be found at the rear of the book.

CONTENTS

1 North Snowdonia & Caernarfon

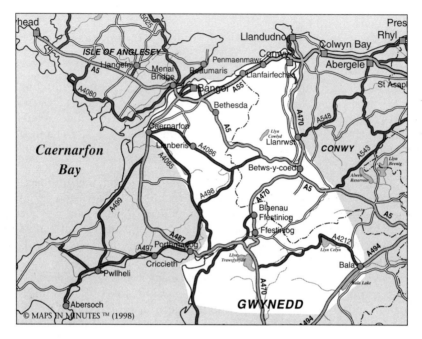

Wales, though part of the United Kingdom, is sometimes mistakenly considered to be a western extension of England. Nothing could be further from the truth as Wales has a long and colourful history of its own and many parts have remained fiercely independent for generations. With Celtic ancestry rather than Anglo-Saxon, the culture of Wales has a distinct flavour of its own and, is obviously, linked with the language.

Geographically speaking, Wales is some 160 miles from north to south and some 50 miles east to west. Anglesey and the Lleyn Peninsula project out into the Irish Sea in the northwest creating the northern boundary of the great crescent of Cardigan Bay. As well as having miles upon miles of coastline, some of the most dramatic in Great Britain, this is also a land of mountains, wild moorlands, and deep valleys.

There are many aspects of North and Mid Wales, from the Eisteddfod and its language to the mining industry and farming, and a great deal to explore. The attraction of Snowdonia National Park and many other areas of outstanding natural beauty make this part of the country a must for those who enjoy the open air be it mountains or sandy beaches.

Often still referred to as the Principality of Wales and, from early times until the accession in 1485 of Welshman Henry Tudor to the English throne, Wales was ruled by princes. These include such people as Llewelyn the Great and Llewelyn the Last, who both at one time held all Wales, and Owain Glyndwr who declared himself Prince of Wales. However, it was an event in 1284 that most people will remember. It was then, in Caernarfon, that Edward I conferred the title of Prince of Wales on his new born son. Today, the title is usually held by the heir to the throne and it was in 1969, at Caernarfon Castle, that HM The Queen conferred the title on Prince Charles.

The Welsh culture, in many ways, is typified by the eisteddfod. Originally meant simply as a meeting of bards, it is now seen also as a means of safeguarding the Welsh language and of promoting Welsh culture. A festival of poetry, singing, and music, Llangollen is the home of the annual (held in July) International Music Eisteddfod, whilst the annual National Eisteddfod is held at different venues.

Today's bardic system, which is purely Celtic in origin, was introduced in 1792 by Edward Williams, a self-taught scholar with a passion for ancient manuscripts on Welsh history. In modern Wales, a bard is a poet who has achieved recognition at an eisteddfod. It is the Gorsedd, or Assembly, that administers the National Eisteddfod and maintains the bardic custom and ceremony.

Myths and legends abound in Wales and many live on in the *Mabinogion*, the creation of the bards of the Dark Ages. Making free with their imagination and with little regard for historical facts, the earliest known written stories can be found in the *White Book of Rhydderch* (1300-25) and the *Red Book of Hergest* (1375-1425). The Mabinogion was translated, in 1838, by Lady Charlotte Guest, wife of a Merthyr Tydfil ironmaster. King Arthur features greatly in Welsh legends; he slew a giant and was mortally wounded on Snowdon and a number of burial chambers bear his name (though they date from 2000 years before his death!)

Of the three National Park in Wales, Snowdonia, at some 840 square miles, is the largest and scenically most dramatic. Embracing several mountain ranges, the National Park takes its name from Snowdon (3,560 feet), the highest mountain in England and Wales. However, the park's name is misleading as it suggests that it covers just the area around the mountain when, in fact, Snowdonia extends southwards into central Wales, all the way to Machynlleth.

In the north Snowdonia is rugged and mountainous, with the glaciated valleys and volcanic peaks around Snowdon gaining most of the attention. Around the popular centre of Betws-y-Coed there is gentler forest walking and those looking for open hillsides make for the unexplored Aran and Arennig mountains around Bala.

There are several routes up to the summit of Snowdon, all beginning at various points around its base. For the less energetic, ascent to the summit can be made by the Snowdon Mountain Railway from Llanberis. This unique, narrow gauge, rack and pinion railway was opened in 1896 and the journey, which is popular throughout the year, takes an hour.

CAERNARFON

Situated on the right bank of the River Seiont, near the southwest end of the Menai Strait, Caernarfon is a town steeped in history. In particular, Caernarfon is famous for its impressive castle ruins that rise above this compact town. Begun in 1283 by Henry de Elreton - who also built Beaumaris Castle - under orders from Edward I, the castle took some 40 years to complete. The plan of **Caernarfon Castle** is of two oval-shaped courts divided by a wall. The outer defences are at intervals strengthened

Caernarfon Castle

by towers and are, in places, 15 feet thick! Many attempts were made by the Welsh, over the years, to destroy the castle but their failure is confirmed by the presence of this magnificent building today. The **Museum of the Royal Welsh Fusiliers** can be found in the Queen's Tower within the castle and, in 1969, the dramatic ruins were used as the location of the investiture of Prince Charles as Prince of Wales.

The history of the town goes back to Roman times and **Segontium Roman Fort**, half a mile out of the town on the Beddgelert road, has a museum containing pottery, weapons, and other items found on the site as well as displays covering Roman military life in general. It is believed that Constantine the Great was born at the fort. Close by is **Llanbedlig Church**, built in the 13th century on an ancient Roman site which used to be a shrine to the god Mithras. To the east of the town, on **Twt Hill**, there is evidence of a Celtic settlement.

The castle sits where the River Seinot meets the Menai Strait which separates mainland Wales from the Isle of Anglesey. Close by, the old Slate Quay, from which slate was once shipped, is now the place from which to book fishing trips or pleasure cruises up the Strait to Beaumaris. Castle Square, on the landward side of the castle, holds markets on Saturdays and contains statues of two famous Welshmen: the gesticulating, urging Lloyd George, once MP for the area, and Sir Hugh Owen, the founder of Further Education in Wales.

The Anglesey Hotel and the **Hanging Tower** stand by the castle walls and were a customs house until 1822. The last hanging to take place in the tower was in 1911 when an Irishman, named Murphy, was executed for murdering a maid. It is said that when he died the bell clapper in **St Mary's Church** fell off. The church itself was founded in 1307 and, though much of it has since been reconstructed, the arcades of the eastern and southern walls are part of the original 14th-century building.

Situated in Castle Street opposite Caernarfon Castle's entrance, **The Castell Restaurant** is an attractive and welcoming establishment that is housed in a delightful Georgian building. Owned and personally run by Irene Austerberry since 1994, the restaurant has gained an enviable reputation locally for their delicious, home-cooked dishes. Nicely decorated and furnished throughout, with a splendid mural of the castle and several prints of local landmarks displayed on the walls and a display of crockery in the bar area, this is an elegant and friendly place that the whole family will enjoy. Open every day from noon until the evening, and split between the

The Castell Restaurant, 6 Castle Street, Caernarfon, Gwynedd LL55 1SE Tel: 01286 674656

ground and first floor, there is an extensive and varied menu where everything is freshly prepared and cooked to order. This is supplemented by an array of ever changing daily specials and there are also dishes specially prepared for children. A popular choice for the people of Caernarfon and the surrounding area, it is advisable to book a table at the weekend to avoid disappointment.

The Hole in the Wall Inn, Hole in the Wall Street, Caernarfon, Gwynedd LL55 1RF Tel: 01286 672694

The Hole in the Wall Inn is one of the oldest, if not the oldest, drinking establishment in Caernarfon and it can be found right by the castle walls. There has been an inn on this site since the mid-15th century and it is believed that the first pub was built at the same time as the Porth Mawr Gateway. The inn takes its name from the large hole in the castle walls through which food was passed to the town's beggars. Today, The Hole in the Wall is run by Helen and Brian Hughes and this popular inn not only has a lovely olde worlde character but also some fine ales to match. There is always a good selection of draught real ales, stouts, lagers, and ciders to choose from and there is plenty of comfortable seating. Open all day, every day, the Tuesday and Sunday evening Kareoke and sing-alongs are very popular. A warm welcome is extended to all who visit this friendly pub, including children.

In the centre of the town, not far from the castle walls lies **Pablo's Gallery**, an Aladdin's cave for those interested in paintings and local crafts. Owned and personally run by two professional artists, Clare Roberts and Stephen Jones, all the work on display is produced by artists and craftsmen and women from the Caernarfon area and Anglesey. Both Stephen's fantasy paintings of Welsh history and dragons, as well as blue's singers, and Clare's work, chiefly silk and oil paintings, are on display. There are a mass of cards, prints, and objet d'art too that are

Pablo's Gallery, 7 High Street, Caernarfon, Gwynedd LL55 1RN Tel: 01286 675737

sure to catch the eye. Open every day in the summer season and on Saturdays throughout the winter, this gallery is sure to have something of interest for everyone whatever their taste and pocket.

Northgate Street is called, in Welsh, Stryd Pedwar a Chewch - meaning four and six street. Apparently it originates from the time when sailors flocked to this part of the town looking for lodgings: four pence for a hammock and six pence for a bed. From the town, on newly opened track, the world famous Ffestiniog Railway runs a service to Dinas Junction. This is the beginning of a project that will eventually see the reopening of a longer stretch of the **Welsh Highland Railway**, from Caernarfon through to Porthmadog, where it will join with the existing Ffestiniog line.

Within easy walking distance of the centre of Caernarfon, the **Menai Bank Hotel** is a wonderful, family hotel that offers not only excellent hospitality but also magnificent views over the Menai Straits to Anglesey. Formerly two late Victorian houses, the building, which is owned and personally run by Liz and Tony Cox, has retained many of its original features including ornate cornices, marble and decorated slate fireplaces, and stained glass windows.

As with any house of this age, the rooms are both spacious and well proportioned and the hotel offers its guests comfortable accommodation in a choice of 15 superb rooms, most of which have en-suite facilities.

Menai Bank Hotel, North Road, Caernarfon, Gwynedd LL55 1BD
Tel: 01286 673297

However, a good night's sleep is not all that guests at the Menai Bank Hotel can expect because Liz's culinary skills are well known throughout the area and the meals here are a treat worth savouring. The restaurant, which is also open to non-residents for whom booking is recommended, is a popular local eating place and will certainly add greatly to guest's enjoyment. Closed for November, this warm and friendly hotel offers all who stay here a relaxing break and children, who will also make good use of the hotel garden, are welcome.

Found just outside Caernarfon, at Pontrug, **Seiont Nurseries** was established in the late 1970s on the site of an old woollen mill, which is still standing. Covering some 35 acres in all, though the majority of the area is used for the cultivation of the wide range of plants, this privately owned concern also has an attractive and well laid out Garden Centre. Open

Seiont Nurseries, Caer Glyddyn, Pontrug, near Caernarfon, Gwynedd LL55 2BB Tel: 01286 672524/672113 Fax: 01286 677223

throughout the year, not only are the majority of the plants and shrubs for sale here home-grown but there is also a vast array of gardening equipment and other items on display.

Spread out over three acres, the outdoor area of the garden centre has been carefully planned to enable customers to see the plants as well as easily find their way around. For those in need of a little guidance on a particular plant or with a tricky gardening issue, the helpful and friendly staff are always on hand with advise. Through the centre also runs the old Caernarfon to Llanberis railway, which, though at the moment disused, plans to be reopened and a miniature railway run along part of its length. Finally, to the rear of the nursery is a beautifully landscaped caravan and camping site complete with a modern shower and toilet block. Open from March to October, the site is surrounded by mature trees and has a river running along one side.

EAST OF CAERNARFON

BANGOR   Map 2 ref F3
8 miles NE of Caernarfon on A487

This is the largest town in northwest Wales and it lies at the foot of a valley besides the Menai Strait. A monastic community was founded here in 525 by St Deiniol, some 70 years before Canterbury, and the town's name is derived from the wattle fence which surrounded St Deiniol's primitive enclosure - 'bangori' is still used in parts of Wales to describe the plaiting of twigs in a hedge. The oldest bishopric in Britain, Bangor's **Cathedral** dates back to the 13th century and has probably been in continuous use for longer than any other cathedral in Britain. Restored in 1866 by Gilbert Scott, the cathedral contains a life-size carving of Christ dating from 1518, the tomb of Owain Glyndwr, and, in the close, is a Biblical garden, containing plants associated with the Bible and the medieval church.

Bangor itself was little more than a village until the slate boom in the 19th century. The nearby Penrhyn Quarry had docks built here and the town flourished in its new role to become a commercial centre. Its importance increased when the **University College of North Wales** was founded here in 1884.

The **Victorian Pier**, built in 1896, stretches out into the Menai Strait and, as well as being a fetching construction, is a pleasant place from which to view Snowdonia, the coast, the busy lanes of small boats passing by, and admire the houses, some magnificent, that stand by the Menai Strait. Pleasure and fishing trips can be taken from the pierhead.

Pier at Bangor

Back in the town centre, the **Museum of Welsh Antiquities and Art Gallery**, housed in the Old Canonry, contains exhibits of period costume and furniture, the most complete Roman sword in Wales, and mementoes of the great engineer, Thomas Telford.

The **Menai Suspension Bridge** was built by Thomas Telford between 1819 and 1826 and it was the first permanent crossing of the Menai Strait. Before its completion the crossing had been made by ferry, and cattle, on their way to and from market, had had to swim the Strait. Not surprisingly there was much opposition to the construction not only from the ferrymen but also from ship-owners worried that the structure would impede the passage of their tall ships. As a result of this concern, the road bridge stands at a height of 100 feet. The **Britannia Bridge**, a mile further southwest from Telford's bridge, is a combined road and rail bridge and was built between 1846 and 1850 by Robert Stephenson.

Penrhyn Castle is a splendid Victorian building that was financed, in 1827, by GH Dawkins, the owner of the Penrhyn Slate Quarry in Bethesda. From the outside it is reminiscent of Norman architecture whilst the interior is decorated, at times overwhelmingly opulently, with a variety of styles as well as materials which seem to occupy every available piece of space. There is a collection of Old Masters in the dining and breakfast rooms and in the restored stableblock is the **Industrial Railway Museum**. The gardens are attractive to wander round as well as giving good views of Snowdonia and the coast.

Situated in the heart of Bangor, opposite the University, **The Ffesant and Firkin** is a popular town centre pub whose attractive black and white exterior is hard to miss. The building dates from the late 18th century but

The Ffesant and Firkin, Glanrafon, Bangor, Gwynedd LL57 1LH
Tel: 01248 351037

the pub has only recently taken its present name and was, for many years, known as The Old Glan. Managed today by Darryll Shields, The Ffesant and Firkin not only received a new name in 1996 but also a complete refurbishment and is now, with the wooden floors and exposed beams, a cosy and traditional pub with a warm and welcoming atmosphere. Open all day, every day, the pub is owned by the Firkin Brewery and, naturally, there is a fine selection of these ales, along the others, behind the bar. Food too is available here until the early evening and the menus, along with the ever changing specials board, offer an excellent choice of tasty snacks and meals. The Ffesant and Firkin is not only the place for good food, drink, and company but there is also a plenty of entertainment laid on for customers to enjoy: Thursday evening is quiz night, a large screen television shows the best of the premier football matches, and live bands perform here on Wednesday evenings.

Situated near to Bangor's bus station, **The Coach House** is an attractive and pleasant café that has been owned and personally run by Gwenda Kotkowicz since 1997. Following a complete refurbishment, this popular café offers customers a comprehensive and varied menu throughout the day in a comfortable and charming atmosphere that is both welcoming and friendly. Open all day, every day except Sundays, The Coach House has something for everyone, whatever the time of day. Assisted by her daughter Sarah, Gwenda has certainly turned the fortunes of this café round in a very short space of time and it is definitely the place to come to for a tasty snack or light meal.

The Coach House, Llys Gwynedd, Fford Gwynedd, Bangor,
Gywnedd LL57 1DT Tel: 01248 371178

Found just outside Bangor, on the road to Caernarfon, **Ty Golchi** is a well known and highly regarded restaurant and tea rooms that has been owned and personally run by Gwyn Jones since 1995. Housed in the a delightful building which dates back to 1840, Ty Golchi, which translates as Wash House, is situated in its own lovely gardens. Open throughout the day, customers can enjoy a varied menu that ranges from breakfasts

Ty Golchi, Caernarfon Road, Vaynol Roundabout, Bangor, Gwynedd LL57 4BT Tel: 01248 671542

through morning coffee to tasty lunches and afternoon teas. Pleasantly decorated and comfortably furnished, the restaurant has a warm and friendly atmosphere and, especially welcome in the summer, is the patio area overlooking the flower filled beds in the garden. A superb place for delicious food any time during the week, the traditional Sunday lunch, for which booking is advised, is particularly popular.

BETHESDA   MAP 2 REF F3
9 miles E of Caernarfon off A5

Often considered the 'Gateway to Snowdonia', this old quarry town takes its name from the Nonconformist chapel that began here and which served many of the 2,300 men who worked in the quarry at its peak in 1875, and their dependants. The gouged rock of the **Penrhyn Slate Quarries** forms a hugh hillside amphitheatre and it was the largest open cast slate mine in the world.

From the town, the main road travels through the beautiful **Nant Ffrancon Pass** which runs straight through and up the valley of the River Ogwen and into the Snowdonia National Park.

LLANBERIS   MAP 2 REF F4
6 miles E of Caernarfon on A4086

This town, perched on the mountainside, has many attractions to keep

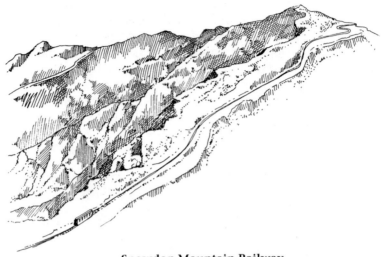

Snowdon Mountain Railway

the visitor occupied. However, Llanberis is perhaps most well known for the nearby mountain, **Snowdon**, and the rack and pinion **Snowdon Mountain Railway** which from here climbs to the summit. Built in 1896, the train has taken millions up to the top where, on a clear day, the views are astonishing. The footpath, that begins close by the railway terminus and passes by a waterfall, is considered the easiest of the three routes up to Snowdon's 3,560 foot summit.

It is not surprising that this mountainous and inhospitable area is also steeped in legend and mystery. The eagles of Snowdon have long been regarded as oracles of peace and war, triumph and disaster, and Snowdon's peak is said to be a cairn that was erected over the grave of a giant killed by King Arthur.

For those wanting another train ride or who are content with a more sedate journey, the **Llanberis Lake Railway** takes a 40-minute trip during which there are different views of the mountain. The railway lies in **Parc Padarn**, where there is the opportunity to visit the **Welsh Slate Museum** in what was the Dinorwic Slate Quarry. Nearby, the **Quarry Hospital** is a restored quarrymen's hospital where the medical facilities available for workers of the time are on display. There are also several trails that skirt Llyn Padarn and the surrounding woodlands with picnic sites in pleasant locations.

Renowned throughout the area for its imaginative cuisine, **Y Bistro** is an excellent restaurant found in the heart of Llanberis. Proprietors Danny and Nerys Roberts have been here for 20 years and they form the perfect partnership with Nerys, who has been in catering all her life, mastermind-

Y Bistro, 43-45 Stryd Fawr, Llanberis, Gwynedd LL55 4EU
Tel & Fax: 01286 871278

ing the superb menus and Danny being a friendly front of house host. In the last few years, their daughter Rhian and son-in-law Siôn have joined them.

Built in the 1860s, Y Bistro has had a varied history and has in its time been the public library and even the labour exchange. Today, it is beautifully decorated to provide a cosy and intimate setting in which to savour Nerys' and Siôn's culinary creations which make the very best use of seasonal fresh vegetables, local meats, fish, and game. The menus change most days and include dishes such as rack of lamb with herb crust and sloe sauce, cockles and samphire in beer batter, and brown sugar hazelnut meringues. The comprehensive wine list boasts over 80 bins.

The last Friday of the month sees the popular theme nights, for which bookings are advisable, as they are for other nights. For superb Welsh cuisine, with a hint of continental flavour, Y Bistro is just the place for those who appreciate good food served in pleasant surroundings. Those who dine here will not be surprised to learn that the restaurant has won many accolades and is regularly featured in all the major food guides.

Opposite the hospital is the **Power of Wales**, a comprehensive exhibition concerned with the history of Welsh industry. Visitors are guided through the centuries and it soon becomes apparent at the great contribution made by this country during the Industrial Revolution. There is also the opportunity to see **Dinorwic Power Station**, a pumped storage hydro-electric power station built into the mountain where tours take visitors into tunnels and the machinery rooms that control this major feat of engineering.

In such a rugged setting, where life has always been harsh, it comes as no surprise to find that it is said that the strongest woman to have ever lived came from Llanberis. Born in 1696, Marged vch Ifan died at the ripe old age of 105. At 70, it was said, she could out wrestle any man in Wales and could also catch as many foxes in one year as the local huntsmen in ten. After receiving many offers of marriage, Marged is said to have chosen the smallest and most effeminate of her suitors. Tradition has it that she only beat her husband twice: after the first beating he married her and after the second he became an ardent churchgoer!

The **Pass of Llanberis** is one of the most desolate passes in Wales and is dominated by Snowdon to the south and the curiously-shaped **Glyder Fawr's** 3,279 feet. Sheep straddle the narrow road which, in some places, is almost blocked by boulders and rocks.

The remains of **Dolbadarn Castle**, a 13th-century Welsh stronghold of Llewelyn the Great, lie beside the road as it leaves the pass and descends into Llanberis. Guarding the pass and overlooking Llyn Padarn, the main feature of the castle is its circular keep.

LLANRUG   MAP 1 REF E4
3 miles E of Caernarfon on A4086

There are many places to visit in the lowland area around the village of Llanrug but one of the most impressive is **Bryn Bras Castle**. Regarded as a 19th-century piece of romanticism, the castle is thought to be the work of Thomas Hopper who was also involved in the building of Penrhyn Castle. Visitors are welcome to look round the interior but perhaps more impressive is its setting within 32 acres of lawns and gardens with trails leading through mature woodland.

In the heart of **Bethel**, a village just north of Llanrug, lies **Y Bedol**, an excellent country inn that was purpose built by the owners, Carolynne and Kevin Johnson, in the late 1980s. Although the building is modern, the interior decor, atmosphere, and hospitality offered by the couple is very much in keeping with the traditions of an old village pub. Beamed ceilings, leaded windows, and a mass of pictures and prints on the walls all add to the charming and delightful character of Y Bedol. Popular with local people, the pub serves a fine array of real ales as well as the usual beers, stouts, and lagers and it is also an excellent place to eat. There is a varied and comprehensive menu available with a choice of dishes to suit

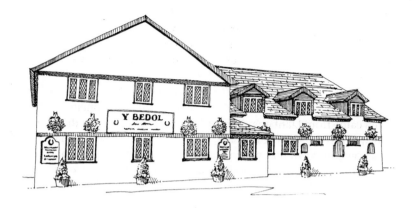

**Y Bedol, Bethel, near Caernarfon, Gwynedd LL55 1AX
Tel: 01248 670155**

every taste and pocket for both lunch and dinner. It is always best to book a table at the weekend, particularly for Sunday lunchtime. One further added attraction at this superb place is the live music each Friday and Saturday evening that draws people from far and wide.

BETWS-Y-COED

This overgrown, sprawling village on the banks of the River Llugwy, just above its confluence with the River Conwy, lies in the Snowdonia National Park and on the edge of the **Gwydyr Forest Park**. In such a super position, it is not surprising that Betws-y-Coed has become a bustling holiday centre. From humble beginnings, Betws-y-Coed (the name means Chapel in the Woods) began to grow with the coming of the railways which helped to develop the village into a popular inland holiday town in Victorian times. The Old Church, near the railway station, has been in use since the 14th century and remained the town's major place of worship until the New Church was built in the 19th century.

Close to the point where the Conwy, Lledr, and Llugwy rivers meet, it is not surprising that these waterways play an important part in the development, building, and beauty of the town. Thomas Telford's **Waterloo Bridge**, a marvellous iron construction, built in 1815, gracefully spans the River Conwy, while the **Pont-y-Pair**, dated around 1470, crosses the River Llugwy and, further downstream, an iron suspension footbridge crosses by the church. Probably the main attraction that draws people to the area are the waterfalls, the Swallow, Conwy Falls, and Fairy Glen Ravine.

However, though water has played an important part in the life of the town, **Betws-y-Coed Motor Museum** caters for those who like their transport to come with four wheels. This unique collection of vintage and classic cars and vehicles was started by the Houghton Family and can be found beside the River Llugwy in an old stone building. With over 30 vehicles on display, including rare and exotic Bugattis and Aston Martins, the museum is sure to be of great interest to all. Railway buffs too are catered for in Betws-y-Coed and they will find a visit to the **Conwy Valley Railway Museum**, adjacent to the town's station, pleasurable. As well as the numerous displays there are steam train and tram rides for the whole family to enjoy.

Perhaps the town's most famous, and certainly most curious, building is **Ty Hyll**, the Ugly House, which stands close to the River Llugwy. Apparently this building, which looks literally looks like it has been thrown together, is an example of hurried assembly in order to obtain freehold on common land. The house was often used as an overnight stop by Irish drovers taking cattle to English markets.

AROUND BETWS-Y-COED

CAPEL GORMAN   Map 2 ref G4
2 miles SE of Betwys-Y-Coed off the A5

Just to the southeast of Betws-y-Coed lies the tiny village of **Capel Garmon**. Surrounded by the spectacular scenery of the Snowdonia mountain range, this delightful place lies within easy reach of historic Conwy and the many lovely Welsh coastal resorts. For the superstitious visitor, an additional attraction has to be the two legends associated with the village inn. The first involves the daughter of a long-ago owner of the inn, who fell in love with a local farm hand. One night he rode up on his white horse and she climbed down from her bedroom window and rode off with him, never to be seen again. The second is apparently a friendly blonde lady who watches over all the events here, but no one knows for sure whether the two are connected.

Close by the village is the **Capel Garmon Burial Chamber**. Dating from around 1500 BC, the remains of a long barrow with three chambers, one with its capstone still in position, can still be seen.

LLANRWST   Map 2 ref G4
4 miles N of Betws-y-Coed on A470

The town's name is derived from St Grwst (Restitutus), a 6th-century missionary who was active in the area and to whom the church has long been dedicated. The **Church of St Grwst** dates from 1470, though the tower and north aisle are 19th-century constructions, and it replaced a thatched building from 1170 that was destroyed in the fighting of 1468.

Found in the centre of the town, **Pen-y-Bryn Hotel** is a charming old building that dates back to the 17th century. Today, managed by Alan and Joyce, with the help of regular barmaid, Kay Wynn, this is a very popular town pub indeed.

Open all day, every day, this is the place to come to for quality ale served in comfortable and friendly surroundings. Attractively decorated and furnished, during a refurbishment programme in 1994, a beautiful inglenook fireplace was discovered that had been boarded up for many years - it is now a fine feature here. Children are welcome here during the day, either in the rear of the pub's several bar areas, or in the pleasant beer garden and there is

The Pen-y-Bryn Hotel, Ancaster Square,
Llanrwst, Conwy LL26 0LH Tel: 01492 640670

excellent access for the disabled customer. Following on from their success and reputation for offering good quality beer, Alan and Joyce are busy planning the menu for a tasty range of bar snacks and meals.

Gwydir Chapel, next to the church, should not to be confused with **Gwydir Uchaf Chapel** which is found on the opposite side of the river. The latter stands in Gwydir Hill Park and is the private chapel of the Wynn family and houses memorials to this family. Built in 1633 by Sir Richard Wynn the chapel, now with Forestry Commission Offices close by, has an interesting painted ceiling and also contains a stone coffin said to be that of Llewelyn the Great.

Below lies the Tudor **Gwydir Castle**, the Wynn family seat. The castle has a cedar tree, planted in 1627 to commemorate the wedding of Charles I, in its attractive grounds in which peacocks wander on the lawns. An arch also stands here that was built to celebrate the ending of the War of the Roses. Inside there is a secret room, once hidden by a wooden panel, and the ghost of a monk is said to be trapped in the tunnel leading from the arch.

The **Old Bridge**, thought to have been built in 1636 by Inigo Jones, was modified in 1703 when a section was carried away by the swollen river. Next to the bridge stands **Tu Hwnt i'r Bont** (the House over the Bridge), a 15th-century courthouse that has since been divided to make two cottages. Owned by the National Trust, Tu Hwnt i'r Bont is let as a tea room and shop. The Gorsedd stones nearby commemorate the National Eisteddfod held here in 1951.

TREFRIW	MAP 2 REF G4
5 miles N of Betws-y-Coed on B5106	

This village, in the beautiful Conwy Valley, was once one of the homes of Llewelyn the Great. He is said to have built a church here to please his wife who refused to climb to the nearest church at Llanrhychyrn. Today, Trefriw is noted for its two main attractions: **Trefriw Woollen Mill** and the local chalybeate springs. The woollen mill has been in production since the 1830s and visitors can view all the processes in the manufacture of tapestries and tweeds from raw wool.

Sometime between AD 100 and AD 250, whilst prospecting for minerals in the area, the Romans opened up a cave where they found a chelybeate (rich in iron) spring. Later covered by a landslide, the cave was reopened in the 18th century by Lord Willoughby de Eresby who also built and exploited a stonework bathhouse. Taking the waters here became so popular that, by 1874, a Victorian pumphouse and bath had been built and the bottled waters were sold worldwide. After a period of decline, the recent interest in natural remedies has turned around the fortunes of the spring.

Dating back to 1652 and standing in its own private and extensive grounds with glorious views over the Conwy valley, **Hafod Country Hotel** offers customers the very best in hospitality. Originally a long house, Hafod means a summer dwelling, this hotel has been owned and personally run by Rosina and Chris Nichols since 1997 and they have created a distinctive retreat with excellent food to match. There are seven magnificent guest rooms, all of which have en-suite facilities, but all of which are individually decorated and furnished in a stylish and comfortable manner. The ideal place for a relaxing night's sleep the beds are as individual as the rooms and are a feature in themselves - be it a fine brass bedstead or a luxurious half tester. The lounge, with its roaring log fire, bar, and restaurant are also imaginatively and stylishly furnished and the atmosphere in the hotel is more that of a rambling farmhouse than of a formal country home.

Chris is the chef of the partnership and food certainly lies at the heart of the Hafod Country Hotel. Every dish is especially prepared from the

**Hafod Country Hotel, Trefriw, near Llanrwst, Conwy LL27 0RQ
Tel: 01492 640029 Fax: 01492 641351**

freshest of local ingredients and presented in a manner that makes dining here a most enjoyable experience. A delicious mix of traditional, European, Mediterranean and old fashioned cuisine, the menu is a delight to read and provides an interesting and varied choice. Open to non-residents, it is best to book to avoid disappointment as this is a small, intimate, and popular restaurant. Children over 11 years of age are welcome at Hafod Country Hotel which is open all year except for January and early February.

TYN-Y-GROES

MAP 2 REF G3

10 miles N of Betws-y-Coed on B5106

Before bridges were built spanning the Conwy estuary people crossed the river from here to Tal-y-cafn and **Bodnant Gardens**, now owned by the National Trust, lie on the other side of the river, just off the main road.

These gardens were first laid out by Henry Pochin in 1875 and are claimed to be amongst the finest in the world. Decoration is an important factor at Bodnant and the many fountains, ornaments, and balustrades blend in with the surroundings. Laid out in two parts, the upper garden around the house is terraced and the lower, known as The Dell, is formed round the River Hiraethlyn, a tributary of the Conwy. The pretty Garden House was built in Gloucestershire in the 1730s and was later used as a Pin Mill before being bought to Bodnant in 1938. It now stands attractively at the end of a pool. The gardens are open to the public from March to

October and the flora in bloom depends, naturally, upon the time of year. In March and April daffodils amongst other spring blossoms sprinkle the grounds. Azaleas, rhododendrons, magnolias and camellias bloom from March to June. There is a laburnum arch which is best seen in June, whilst in the terraces all kinds of herbaceous borders flourish.

Just to the south, at **Tal-y-Bont**, lies **The Lodge Hotel** one of the area's most popular hotels and restaurants which has, over a number of years, established a fine reputation for the high standard of hospitality it offers all its guests. Built in the 1970s on the site of a small holding, not only is

The Lodge Hotel, Tal-y-Bont, Conwy LL32 8YX
Tel: 01492 660766 Freephone 0800 917 6593 Fax: 01492 660534
e-mail: bbaldon@lodgehotel.co.uk www.lodgehotel.co.uk

the building a place of friendliness and comfort but its position within extensive and attractive grounds adds to the air of relaxation and tranquillity.

Owned and personally run by Barbara and Simon Baldon since the 1980s, the hotel has gained a long list of patrons who return here time and time again. Each of the en-suite guest rooms has been individually styled and decorated to offer the perfect sanctuary for a good night's sleep and all are on the ground floor with patio doors straight into the interesting and well tendered gardens. Food too plays a very important part in the life of The Lodge Hotel and the restaurant is a cosy, informal room with soft lighting to create an intimate atmosphere. Simon, the chef of the partnership, creates a delicious menu using only the very best of local produce and dining here is certainly a treat not to be missed. Open every day except Monday lunchtime, and also to non-residents, booking is essential as this restaurant is well known and highly popular throughout this part of Wales.

ROWEN
MAP 2 REF G3

10 miles N of Betws-y-Coed off B5106

From this quiet village a track, that was once a Roman road, skirts by the foot of **Tal-y-Fan**, which climbs to 2,000 feet at its peak. Roughly six miles in length, the path passes by an ancient burial chamber and eventually drops down toward the coast at Aber.

Just east of the village lies **Parc Glyn** which offers visitors the opportunity not only to see a traditional Welsh farm but also some rare farm animals. Along with the sheep, cattle, and pigs, there are flocks of peacocks, guinea fowl, ducks, and geese and, surrounding the paddocks, in the mixed woodland, are badgers, polecats, squirrels, and a mass of birdlife.

CONWY
MAP 2 REF G3

14 miles N of Betws-y-Coed on A55

On the south bank of the Conwy Estuary, Conwy lies opposite Deganwy. Since the completion of the tunnel carrying the A5 under the estuary, Conwy has returned to something of its former self. No longer harassed by heavy traffic, the town is a delight to wander in: its small streets steeped in history and dominated by another of Edward I's castles. The ruins are eye-catching and it is one of the most picturesque of Wales' many fortresses. In superb condition, **Conwy Castle** is situated on a rock that overlooks the River Conwy and its estuary and commands wonderful views of the whole area. Begun in 1283, the castle's construction was largely finished by the autumn of 1287. The town was walled as well and today the walls still encircle the vast majority of Conwy. The castle itself was built to be suitable as a Royal residence and, in fact, was used twice by Edward I; once on his way to Caernarfon where his son, the first English Prince of Wales, was born and, again, in 1294, when trying to put down the rebellion of Madoc ap Llewelyn.

Later, in 1399, Richard II stayed at the castle before being lured out and ambushed by the Earl of Northumberland's men on behalf of Henry Bolingbroke, the Duke of Lancaster who later became Henry IV. Conwy was given the attention of Owain Glyndwr during his rebellion: his men burnt the town down. As with other castles further east, Conwy was embroiled in the Civil War. A Conwy man, John Williams, became Archbishop of York and, as a royalist, sought refuge in his home town. Repairing the crumbling fortifications at his own expense, Archbishop Williams finally changed sides after shabby treatment by royalist leaders and helped the Parliamentary forces lay siege to the town and castle which eventually fell to them in late 1646.

The town developed within the shadows of its now defunct fortress, and slate and coal, extracted from the surrounding area, was shipped up and down the coast from Conwy. Later, the town fathers approached Thomas Telford who planned a causeway and bridge as the town's trade and links with the outside world increased. Until then the crossing of the estuary had been by ferry or via a bridge further up the river at **Tal-y-cafn**. The scheme was approved and completed by 1826 at a cost of £50,000. The suspension road bridge, its design sympathetic to its surroundings, was soon followed by construction of railways. This time Robert Stephenson designed a tubular rail bridge, by the side of Telford's construction, in 1846. Both builders breached the town walls in styles that complemented the architecture. The structures still stand today to be admired by the visitor.

Plas Mawr, an Elizabethan town house found on High Street, is one of the best preserved buildings from that period in Britain. Built by the influential merchant Robert Wynn between 1576 and 1585 the house, which has been wonderfully preserved, has an interesting stone façade and some 52 windows. Particularly noted for its fine and elaborate plaster ceilings, Plas Mawr (the name means great hall) came into the possession of the Mostyn family during the 18th century and, in 1991, was given, by Lord Mostyn, to the nation. Close by is **Aberconwy House**, a structure dating from the 14th century. This delightful medieval house is open to visitors and each room has been decorated and furnished to reflect a period in the house's long history.

Plas Mawr, Conwy

Occupying part of the site of a 12th-century Cistercian Abbey, which was moved to Maenan by Edward I, is **St Mary's Church**. This abbey church then became the parish church of the borough created by Edward and some interesting features still remain from that time though there have been many additions over the centuries.

The **Teapot Museum**, on Castle Street, is an interesting and unusual attraction. The collection contains teapots from the mid 1700s to the present day and the museum shop sells many varieties of tea as well as related paraphernalia.

It is not surprising that the town and the surrounding area have strong links with the sea and Conwy also has a traditional mermaid story. Washed ashore by a violent storm in Conwy Bay, a mermaid begged the local fishermen who found her to carry her back to the sea. The fishermen refused and, before she died, the mermaid cursed the people of the town, swearing that they would always be poor. In the 5th century, Conwy suffered a fish famine and many said that the cursed was fulfilled.

St Brigid is concerned with another fish famine story. Walking by a riverside carrying some rushes, she threw the rushes upon the water. A few days later the rushes had turned into fish and ever since they have been known as sparlings or, in Welsh, brwyniaid, which both mean 'rush-like'.

On the quayside the fishermen still land their catches and from here pleasure boat trips can be taken. Nearby, in between terraced housing, can be found what is claimed to be **Britain's Smallest House**; its dimensions of 6 feet wide and 10 feet high perhaps confirming that.

PENMAENMAWR   Map 2 ref F3
14 miles N of Betws-y-Coed on A55

This small holiday resort, with its sand and shingle beach, has changed little since William Gladstone holidayed here in the last century. Overlooking Conwy Bay, the town has many fine Victorian buildings.

In the town's steep mountain-backed hinterland can be found many prehistoric sites including one of Wales' best known Bronze Age stone circles, **Cefn Coch**. An urn was uncovered here containing the remains of a child as well as a bronze dagger which is said to be evidence of a ritual sacrifice that once took place on this site.

Standing in the centre of Penmaenmawr, on a once busy road, **The Mountain View Hotel** is now, thanks to the A55 by pass, a hidden place well worth seeking out. Owned and personally run by Jean and Roy Wilson since 1993, this attractive hotel is once again a popular place for all round hospitality. Built over 200 years ago, the building was once a sawmill but today it is comfortable hotel offering customers the very best in food, drink, and accommodation. The bar is popular with both locals and residents alike and there is always a choice of at least four different bitters, as well as the usual drinks, behind the bar. The food too is of the same high quality and, available throughout the day, there is a comprehensive and varied menu supplemented by the list of daily specials. As a family orien-

**The Mountain View Hotel, Pant-yr-Afon, Penmaenmawr, Gwynedd
LL34 6AA Tel: 01492 623446**

tated pub, children are also made welcome. The cosy and well equipped
guest rooms can be taken on a bed and breakfast basis and there are two
family rooms available. Finally, The Mountain View Hotel hosts live entertainment every Friday evening and at most weekends. There is also a
children's room, games room, and a large screen television showing satellite sports.

CAPEL CURIG   MAP 2 REF F4
5 miles W of Betws-y-Coed on A5

Situated at the junction of the mountain roads to Beddgelert, Llyn Ogwen,
and Bangor, Capel Curig is popular place for climbers and is the home of
the **National Centre for Mountaineering Activities.** Hill walkers and
anglers also use the town as a base and it has many places to stop off
scattered through it.

In the heart of Capel Curig lie **Pinnacle Pursuits**, **Pinnacle Café**, and
Capel Curig Stores and Post Office, a successful business that is owned
and run by mother and son, Vera and Philip Jones. The first of the three
premises, which stand side-by-side, is the General Stores, a typical village
shop, combined with a post office, stocked full of provisions and where
visitors are sure to find those items that they forgot to bring with them.
Next door, Pinnacle Pursuits sells everything in the way of outdoor cloth-

ing and equipment that the walker and camper could possible need. As well as the extensive range of clothing, from boots to anoraks, there are also maps and books on the surrounding area that provide a full range of information.

Pinnacle Pursuits, Pinnacle Café, and Capel Curig Stores and Post Office, Capel Curig, Gwynedd LL24 0EN Tel: 01690 720201

Lastly, there is Pinnacle Café, a popular place with the residents of Capel Curig and those visiting the town. Open all day, the menu begins with breakfast and progresses through to meals with an array of tasty snacks and light meals in between. All this is supplemented with the list of daily specials and there is sure to be something to suit everyone here. Freshly prepared and well presented, those with a sweet tooth should look out for the home-made cakes and fruit pies that are as delicious as they are tempting. Going hand-in-hand with the mouth-watering food the Pinnacle Café also prides itself on its high standard of service and friendly atmosphere.

Tyn-y-Coed Hotel is hard to miss as, right outside the building, there is a magnificent old Yorkshire Rose stagecoach on display. Owned and personally run by Jayne and George Wainwright since the late 1970s, this former coaching inn is a delightful, comfortable hotel that is particularly popular with walkers and ramblers who are making the most of the glorious surrounding countryside. Open all year round, as well as the 13 excellent en-suite guest rooms, there is also a bunkroom available that sleeps five. As well as the splendid accommodation, Tyn-y-Coed Hotel offers customers a range of quality real ales from the bar, which includes an ever changing guest ale and at least two Welsh brews. The bar area,

Tyn-y-Coed Hotel, Capel Curig, Gwynedd LL24 0EE
Tel & Fax: 01690 720331

which features a collection of milk jugs hanging from the exposed ceiling beams, is a pleasant and comfortable place that, over the years, has retained its olde worlde character. Here too, throughout the day during the summer, and at lunchtime and in the evening for the rest of the year, a delicious menu of mouth-watering meals and tasty snacks are served. This is a superb place to stay as well as being an ideal centre for exploring Snowdonia and, those interested in ski-ing may like to know that Jayne is a qualified ski instructor and offers lessons on the nearby dry ski slope.

NANT PERIS   MAP 2 REF F4
12 miles W of Betws-y-Coed on A4086

Once known as Old Llanberis, the village has a simple cruciform church which, in parts, dates back to the 12th century and has a 15th-century roof. The **Well of Peris**, which lies just to the north of the village centre, was, until relatively recently, much visited for its healing properties as well as for wishing. A successful request was said to be signalled by the appearance of a sacred fish.

BEDDGELERT   MAP 2 REF F5
14 miles W of Betws-y-Coed on A4085

This village's setting, surrounded by mountains and, in particular, the 2,568 feet of **Moel Hebog**, is reminiscent of the Swiss Alps. In the 6th century a Celtic monastery was founded here which went on to become one of the foremost religious houses in Wales. Later, in the 12th or 13th century, the monastery was succeeded by a small Augustinian priory founded here by Llewelyn the Great. However, Beddgelert was much more than just a religious centre during medieval times. Its role as a port was made possible by the River Glaslyn which was navigable as far as Pont Aberglaslyn and remained so until the building of the Porthmadog embankment in the early 19th century. Of the Augustinian priory, all that remains now is the village church. The village's name translates to Gelert's Grave and refers to Llewelyn the Great killing his dog Gelert as he believed it had savaged his son. The story goes that the dog, in fact, saved the boy from wolves but nowadays historians put little weight behind the legend. The reputed grave of Gelert is in a meadow just to the south of the village though the stones were apparently erected by a local landlord during the 18th century. To the north is **Beddgelert Forest** where forest trails lead to a pleasant picnic spot.

Sygun Copper Mine, on the Capel Curig road, is an outstanding example of Welsh heritage restored and transformed into a popular and successful tourist attraction. The guided tour leads visitors through a maze of tunnels and large chambers where there are some incredible stalactite and stalagmite formations. Audio commentaries, in four different languages, detail each stage of the mining process, with lighting and sound effects contributing to this fascinating glimpse into the past.

Further along, the road passes through what is often described as the most attractive of mountain passes. Skirting by **Llyn Dinas** this area is associated with Merlin the magician and legend claims that the true throne of Britain is in the lake waiting for the day that a young person standing on a certain stone will reveal it. An ancient fort, Dinas Emrys, once stood to the west of the lake. Behind Llyn Dinas, **Yr Aran** rises to 2,451 feet and its height gives the lake an almost magical appearance. Further on through the pass is **Llyn Gwynant**, which again is quite beautiful as the water weaves its way down the slopes of the 2,030 feet of **Gallt-y-Wenallt**. Close by the Watkins path winds its way through woodland to open country before finally arriving at Snowdon's summit.

Found in the heart of this popular tourist village, **Lyn's Café and Tea Garden** is a very popular place that comes highly recommended by the people of the village. Owned and personally run by Lyn Wheatley, with the help of chef, Julie Burnett, in the years since Lyn first bought the premises, in 1988, its reputation has gone from strength to strength. Open well into the evening seven days a week from February to October and at weekends for the rest of the year, this cosy and attractive café offers customers a varied and extensive menu of light meals and snacks through to a full gourmet dinner. There is also a small but select list of wines and the ever changing daily specials board adds further to the choice for dinner. As well as the delicious home-cooked meals and home-made cakes and

**Lyn's Café and Tea Garden, Church Street, Beddgelert, Gwynedd
LL55 4YA Tel: 01766 890374**

pastries, Lyn's Café has a take-away service and there is also a lovely garden, beside the fast flowing River Glaslyn, where dogs are also welcome. This is an excellent friendly establishment that provides customers with a mouth-watering selection of food whatever the time of day.

The outstanding **River Garden Restaurant and Guest House** is, as its name suggests, close to a picturesque river, with just a quiet road between the charming house and the lovely river garden. A delightful place in the summer, the garden not only contains plenty of seating but also an old brightly painted cart that is filled to the brim with a mass of colourful flowers. The restaurant and guest house itself is owned and personally run by Jo Hughes and Julie Mabbott and comprises three old cottages. The ground floor restaurant is a wonderful olde worlde room with exposed stone walls and a cosy and intimate atmosphere. Open from morning until evening throughout the year, this is a popular eating establishment whose reputation for excellent freshly prepared dishes that incorporated the best of Welsh produce has spread far and wide. Children are also well catered for here and it is always best to book a table at the weekends to avoid disappointment.

However, this is not all this charming establishment has to offer as, upstairs, there are five comfortable, en-suite guest rooms as well as a self-contained flat. Overlooking the village centre and very much part of the

**River Garden Restaurant and Guest House, Caernarfon Road,
Beddgelert, Gwynedd LL55 4UY Tel: 01766 890551**

life of Beddgelert, this is an ideal place to stay whilst exploring this wonderful part of the country.

DOLWYDDELAN   Map 2 ref F4
5 miles W of Betws-y-Coed on A470

Here can be seen the stark remains of **Dolwyddelan Castle** which is unusual amongst Welsh castles in that it was built by native Welsh princes
rather than by either the English or the Normans. Built in around 1170,
possibly by Iorwerth, the father of Llewelyn the Great, it is certain that the
Prince later used the castle as his home. Standing guard over a mountain
pass in this quite dramatic setting, the castle was captured by Edward I's
forces in 1283. In 1488, the place was acquired by Maredudd ap Ievan,
who built the village church which houses his kneeling effigy in brass.
After Maredudd's death the castle fell into ruin and the modern roof and
battlements seen today were added in the 19th century. The remains are
now owned, as are most others in the area, by Cadw (Welsh Historic Monuments) and an exhibition here tells the story of the Welsh princes.

BLAENAU FFESTINIOG

Once the Slate Capital of the world, the slate industry still dominates the
landscape and economy of Blaenau Ffestiniog. Stretching across from the
feet of Manod towards the Moelwyn mountains, the legacy of the slate

industry is to be seen everywhere. From the orderly piles of quarried slate waste reaching up hillsides to the buildings in the town, the material has had a great impact. The industry lives on today in two slate mines. **Llechwedd Slate Caverns** offer the opportunity to visit and see the interiors and conditions of the mines. There are two guided tours which include a ride on Britain's steepest passenger railway. Alternatively there is **Gloddfa Ganol Slate Mine** where digging began in 1818 at, reputedly, the world's largest slate mine. Here there is the chance to see slate being turned into commercial products.

As well as the British Rail service here, Blaenau is also the end, or starting point, of the narrow gauge **Ffestiniog Railway**, that runs through the Vale of Ffestiniog to Porthmadog. Once carrying slate down to be shipped off around the world, the railway has since been renovated by enthusiasts and volunteers. There is a comprehensive service that gives travellers the chance to admire the scenery of the vale on their journey down towards the sea. There are many stopping off points so walkers can take advantage of the **Tan-y-Blwch Country Park** and other beauty spots along the route.

Whilst in the area, the **Ffestiniog Visitor Centre** at First Hydro's power station is a worthwhile visit for those interested in hydro-electric power. Opened by Her Majesty the Queen in 1963, the station consists of reservoirs and underwater passages constructed inside the mountains to generate power. The guided tour explains the station's astonishing construction and there are some fascinating displays and exhibits explaining the origins of electricity and its development.

AROUND BLAENAU FFESTINIOG

FFESTINIOG   MAP 2 REF F5
1 mile S of Blaenau Ffestiniog on A470

Situated above the **Vale of Ffestiniog** between it and the valley of the Cynfal, from here there is a delightful local walk, signposted from the church, to the **Cynfal Falls**, just below the town to the south. Above the falls stands a rock, known locally as Pulpud Huw Llwyd, which recalls a local mystic who preached from here.

MAENTWROG   MAP 2 REF F5
4 miles S of Blaenau Ffestiniog on A496

This peaceful and attractive village of stone houses lies in the wooded Vale of Ffestiniog and is home to the **Plas Tan-y-Bwlch** residential study centre of Snowdonia National Park, from which various nature trails lead. One trail follows a path through a nature reserve which protects some of the original oak woods that once covered much of Wales.

The Grapes Hotel is a wonderful 17th-century coaching inn, although its records show its existence as far back as the 1300s, that is owned and personally run by Gill and Brian Tarbox with the help of their sons, Grant as manager and Jamie as restaurant manager. Once frequented by such notables as Lloyd George and Lily Langtry, The Grapes Hotel has been and is today renowned for its ales, cuisine, hospitality, and accommodation. The warmth of the pitch pine, carved oak, and mahogany interior - with log fires in winter - creates a relaxed atmosphere in which to enjoy not only a drink but a tasty selection of freshly prepared, home-cooked bar

The Grapes Hotel, Maentwrog, Gwynedd LL41 4HN Tel: 01766 590365/590208 Fax: 01766 590654

snacks and meals. Still on the subject of dining, the hotel's also has a superb, recently created restaurant, Eko, that is based on organic foods with dishes taken from around the world. A popular place, it is advisable to book a table here to avoid disappointment. Finally, The Grapes offers guests a relaxing and comfortable night's sleep in a choice of eight excellent en-suite rooms: two of these are cottage units situated in the old brew house. This delightful establishment is well worth a visit and it is an ideal place for a holiday in Snowdonia.

LLANFIHANGEL-Y-TRAETHAU   MAP 2 REF F5
9 miles SW of Blaenau Ffestiniog on A496

A narrow lane climbs out of the village to the small church which, before land reclamation, was an island and now offers good views and a different appreciation of Portmeirion's lovely setting across the estuary. In the churchyard stands a 12th-century stone, its Latin inscription recording that it marks the grave of the mother of the church's builder.

Found beside the main road through the village of **Talsarnau**, just to the east of Llanfihangel-y-traethau, **The Bron Trefor Arms** is an attractive pub which, until the 1970s, was a farmhouse. Dating back, in parts, to the mid-18th century, the main farmhouse and the old milking sheds and churn room have been converted, in an imaginative fashion, to create this delightful pub that is now owned and personally run by Olive and Terry Howard. Open every day, and all day at weekends, this is the place to come to for fine ales, delicious food, and charming hospitality. From the bar, customers can make a choice from a range of well-kept ales, beers, and lagers whilst there is an extensive menu of tasty bar meals and snacks

The Bron Trefor Arms, Talsarnau, Gwynedd LL47 6TA
Tel: 01766 770957

served both at lunchtime and in the evening. This comprehensive list is supplemented by the blackboard display of house specialities and the hard to resist dessert menu. Children too are well catered for as, not only do they have their own menu, but there is also a room set aside for them. A lively place, and one where the locals like to congregate at the end of the day, there is music, either live or disco, each Friday and Saturday evening.

Also situated in the pleasant village of Talsarnau and with panoramic views over the estuary to Portmeirion, **Tremeifion Vegetarian Country Hotel** is the ideal place for a relaxing holiday in friendly environment. Owned and personally run by Maureen and John Jackson, this delightfully situated hotel offers guests a choice of five superb guest rooms that are all individually decorated and furnished and have either a view from the front of the house over the river mouth or overlook the hotel's well tendered gardens. Unusual in that it is an exclusively vegetarian establishment, Maureen, who is a professional and highly experienced vegetarian

Tremeifion Vegetarian Country Hotel, Talsarnau, near Harlech, Gwynedd LL47 6UH Tel: 01766 770491

cook, puts together an evening menu that not only offers a guests a choice but also blends tastes, textures, and colours to create a delicious range of tasty and filling dishes. Breakfast too is a feast and, as with all the food served here, incorporates organically grown wholefoods wherever possible. Non-vegetarians among the guests will certainly not miss their meat. Open all year round, this peaceful and homely establishment has a range of packages to suit all needs and requirements.

HARLECH   MAP 2 REF F6
11 miles S of Blaenau Ffestiniog on A496

Harlech translates to 'Bold Rock' and there is no doubting the fact as the town clings to the land at the foot of its spectacularly sited castle. Another of Edward I's fortifications, **Harlech Castle** was begun in 1283, was completed in 1289, and still dominates the area. One can imagine it in former times when the sea reached to the rocks below.

Like the castles in this part of Wales, Harlech Castle was built as part of a ring to contain the Welsh after Edward's conquest of the country. Its situation close to the sea proved useful during the castle's blockade by Madog and his men in 1294, when supplies transported in from Ireland enabled the 37 men inside to hold fast. If the use of power and strength to impress and intimidate an indigenous population are aided by architecture, then surely Harlech Castle succeeded. Built 200 feet above sea level, its concentric design, with lower outer walls, used the natural defences of its site to emphasise its impregnability. Yet the architect, James of St George, could not have reckoned with the coming of Owain Glyndwr who captured the castle in 1404 and held it for five years, whilst he was using Harlech as his capital.

The song *Men of Harlech* has immortalised the siege during the War of the Roses when the castle was held for the Lancastrian side for seven years finally becoming the last castle to fall in England and Wales to the Yorks in 1468. The last time Harlech Castle saw action was during the Civil War when it was the last castle in Wales to fall to the Parliamentary forces. Views from its ramparts across the Tremadog Bay and the mountainous background are quite magnificent. The town below the castle walls is a pleasant place, busy during the summer and with much to attract the visitor.

Just outside the town is **Morfa Harlech**, a nature reserve with woodland trails, which occupies the flat land between Llanfihangel-y-traethau and Harlech. Also on the outskirts of Harlech, though on higher ground, lies **Coed Llechwedd**, a woodland property given to the National Trust in 1937 in memory of the Irish writer AP Graves.

TRAWSFYNYDD   MAP 2 REF F5
6 miles S of Blaenau Ffestiniog off A470

Situated by a lake of the same name which was developed in the 1930s as part of a hydro-electric scheme the village is now home to a nuclear power station.. Visits to **Trawsfynydd Power Station and Visitor Centre** are popular and make a more unusual day out, with their information packed displays and free guided tours around the plant. A three mile nature trail skirts the lake and information about wild and plant life found along the path can be obtained from the visitor centre.

Close to the power station, down a minor road, are the remains of a small Roman amphitheatre which served as a fort. Later used by the Normans as a motte, **Tomen-y-Mur** is associated with the legendary princes of Ardudwy. The story goes that the prince's men, after a raid into Clwyd, were returning with their bounty and Clwydian women when they were caught by the pursuing men and slain. The women, smitten by their captors, drowned themselves in **Llyn Morwynion** close to Ffestiniog, in preference to returning to Clwyd.

In the village centre is a statue in honour of Hedd Wynn, a poet and shepherd who was awarded the bardic chair at the 1917 Eisteddfod whilst he fought and died in the Flanders fields during World War I.

Found on the main street of this village, **Bodwyn Restaurant and Café** is a charming establishment, with a fine local reputation, that is owned

**Bodwyn Restaurant and Café, Trawsfynydd, Gwynedd LL41 4SF
Tel: 01766 540331**

and personally run by Einir and Gareth Jones. The couple came here in
1996, after Einir had spent 20 years working as a nurse, and today, the café
and separate restaurant are proving a great success. Open from early morning (06.30!) until late afternoon, the café is a delightful place for anything
from a cup of tea to a full breakfast. A delicious selection of home-made
cakes are on display to tempt customers and all the dishes are freshly prepared. As the café closes, the adjacent restaurant opens, and this is, again,
the place to come to for superb home-cooked food. Cosy and intimate,
there is an excellent three course set price menu that is very popular with
both locals and visitors alike. Finally, Einir and Gareth also offer bed and
breakfast accommodation in a comfortable family size en-suite room above
the restaurant. A real home from home with a standard of hospitality that
is second to none.

PENMACHNO MAP 2 REF G4
7 miles NE of Blaenau Ffestiniog on B4406

This delightful village of picturesque stone cottages, set in a wooded valley, lies on the River Machno, from which it takes its name. Not only is
Penmachno surrounded by glorious countryside but it is also situated within
an area that is a stronghold of Welsh culture and here can be found the

traditional **Penmachno Woollen Mill**. Weaving skills have been important in Wales since the times of the ancient Celts and here, in an old mill, the weaving of the 'Penmachno rug' can still be seen on looms that were once powered by the river. As well as learning about the skills of the weaver, visitors can also enjoy a break at the centre's café and browse around the mill shop.

PENTREFOELAS   MAP 2 REF G4
11 miles E of Blaenau Ffestiniog on A5

Once an upland estate village, Pentrefoelas is now becoming known as a focus point for the crafts and skills that were used to maintain the estate. Among the attractions to be found here are a working mill and an Industrial Heritage Trail.

The **Levelinus Stone**, an 8 foot pillar, marks the place where the Prince Llewelyn ap Sisyll of Gwynedd fell in battle in 1203.

Found in the heart of the magnificent countryside of North Wales, **Y Giler Arms Hotel** is a lovely establishment situated in its own extensive grounds that not only contain a lake but through which the River Meddwr runs. Dating back to the 17th century this delightful hotel is owned and personally run by Tracey and Graham Gibson and it is the ideal place for those wanting a relaxing and hospitable place to stay whilst touring the area. Comfortable all year round accommodation is provided in a choice of seven well furnished and decorated rooms, many of which have views of the lake. As well as the traditional slate floored public bar, well used by the local people, there is also a cosy lounge bar, complete with wood burner, where a range of keg and draught beers are served along with a wide selec-

Y Giler Arms Hotel, Rhydlydan, Pentrefoelas, near Betws-y-Coed, Gwynedd LL24 0LL Tel: 01690 770612

tion of whiskeys. The attractive and spacious restaurant with picture windows overlooking the grounds offers an extensive and reasonably priced menu and is popular with both local and visiting families. Fishermen will particularly enjoy their stay at Y Giler Arms Hotel as, not only is the lake well-stocked with common and mirror carp and roach, but there are many local places for trout fishermen. Finally, also in the grounds of the hotel is a small and secluded camping and caravan site, licensed for up to five touring caravans, that has its own facilities. Children and dogs are welcome at the hotel.

FRONGOCH   MAP 2 REF H5
13 miles E of Blaenau Ffestiniog on A4212

Just to the west of the village, close to the reservoir **Llyn Celyn**, is the **National White Water Centre**, a must for those who enjoy facing a series of rapids in a canoe or on a raft. On the banks of the lake lies a memorial stone to a group of local Quakers who, centuries ago, emigrated to America to escape persecution. The modern chapel close by, Chapel Celyn, was built as a reminder of the rural hamlet that was drowned when the reservoir was created in the 1960s. Overlooking Llyn Celyn is **Arenig Fawr,** with, on its 2,800 foot summit, has a memorial to the crew of a Flying Fortress that crashed here in 1943.

Situated on the edge of the Snowdonia National Park, **Rhyd y Defaid Farm**, the home of Olwen and John Davies, is a mixed sheep and cattle farm in the heart of some of the most glorious countryside that Wales has to offer. Built over 300 years ago, this solid stone farmhouse is surrounded

Rhyd y Defaid Farm, Frongoch, near Bala, Gwynedd LL23 7NT
Tel & Fax: 01678 520456

by a lovely, sheltered, well-kept garden and from here, as from many rooms in the house, there are magnificent views. Olwen and John have been providing excellent bed and breakfast accommodation from their charming home for many years and the three letting rooms, each with their own en-suite or private bathroom, are comfortable and cosy. A substantial home-cooked breakfast is served each morning in either the attractive conservatory or the delightful breakfast room, which also features a wonderful Welsh dresser. Those who prefer to cater for themselves need not miss out on this superb location as the couple also have a six berth caravan available for hire in their grounds. An ideal base from which to tour the area, the National White Water Centre is only a mile away, Rhyd y Defaid Farm is well worth a visit.

BALA   MAP 2 REF H5
15 miles E of Blaenau Ffestiniog on A494

This agreeable town, with an attractive High Street which caters for most needs, is a good stopping off point when exploring Snowdonia National Park. Once considered a religious centre Bala was also the home of Reverend Thomas Charles, one of the founders of the methodist movement in Wales in the late 18th century. Though not a native of Bala, Thomas Charles first visited the town in 1778 and finally moved here after marrying, in 1783, a local girl, Sally Jones. Working for the Methodist denomination, Charles saw the great need for Welsh Bibles and other religious books and, joining forces with a printer from Chester, they produced a series of books and pamphlets. A statue to Thomas Charles stands outside Tegid Chapel and was erected in memory of the men who edited the first Welsh Bible and was an instigator of the Bible Society. From the old Theological College for Calvinist Methodists, established in 1837, came the Reverend Michael Jones who took many from Bala in 1853 to Patagonia in South America where they practised their nonconformity free from animosity.

The town was also an important centre for the knitted stocking industry that flourished in the 18th century before the inventions and factory systems of the Industrial Revolution put paid to this established cottage industry. However, Bala, which means the outflow of a river from a lake, dates back to the 14th century and it remains a fine example of a well planned borough. From its beginnings, the town's economy was centred around agriculture and, in 1324, as well as being created a free borough, Bala was granted a charter to hold a weekly market and two annual fairs. Today, through tourism is certainly an important part of the town's economy, Bala has remained a central meeting point and market place for surrounding farming communities.

Bala Lake (Llyn Tegid), the largest natural lake in Wales and feeder of the River Dee, is a major watersports centre and along its banks runs a narrow gauge railway. Traditionally, the old town of Bala lies, drowned, at the bottom of the lake and, so the legend goes, one day the lake will swallow up new Bala too.

Right in the heart of Bala lies **Plas-yn-Dre**, a licensed restaurant that has been in the Williams family since the early 1970s. This superb restaurant is hard to miss with its white and blue painted front and though the building itself dates back to the 16th century, it stands on the site of a dwelling which, in the 12th century, was home to the Welsh prince Rhiddid Flaidid (Richard the Wolf). Personally run by John and Ceri Williams, with the their two sons, Sion and Owain, who are top chefs, Plas-yn-Dre (which means Mansion in the Town) is a popular eating place that has an enviable reputation for its high standard of cuisine and service.

Plas-yn-Dre, High Street, Bala, Gwynedd LL23 7LU
Tel: 01678 521256

Open for both lunch and dinner, there are a variety of menus designed to satisfy the needs of all customers - from light lunches to full evening à la carte and children are also specifically catered for. Whilst this is very much an international restaurant, with Sion and Owain blending flavours from around the world, there is also very much a hint of Wales running through all the menus with great emphasis placed on fresh ingredients and top class presentation. Any meal here, be it a celebration dinner, a light lunch, or one of the summer outdoor barbecues, is a treat for all the family and, with delightful, comfortable surroundings to match, everyone is sure to enjoy their eating experience.

Once found, and **Cwm Hwylfod** certainly classes as a hidden place, this charming old farmhouse is well worth remembering. Found in a sheltered position overlooking the Dee Valley and close to Bala Lake, Cwm Hwylfod, which means valley of happiness, is a 400-year-old sheep farm that used to be an inn at the meeting point of five drovers' routes. Today, this is the home of Joan and Edward Best who offer superb bed and break-

Cwm Hwylfod, Cefn-Ddwyifod, near Bala, Gwynedd LL23 7LN
Tel & Fax: 01678 530310

fast accommodation from their lovely house in a choice of three comfortable guest rooms. With panoramic views over the dramatic surrounding countryside, this is ideal walking country and a number start right from the front door. As well as excellent accommodation, Joan and Edward also serve delicious home-cooked meals, with a variety of special diets catered for including babies and vegans. With a wealth of things to do in the area, this hospitable couple are also happy to supply guests with maps and leaflets relating to this splendid part of Wales, help book pony trekking and water sports in advance, and arrange courses in English as a foreign language at the house.

LLANUWCHLLYN

MAP 2 REF G6

14 miles SE of Blaenau Ffestiniog on A494

At the southern end of Bala Lake, the hamlet is the terminus of the **Bala Lake Railway** and a return trip on this 2 foot gauge railway, from here to Bala, takes one hour. The track follows the lake for four miles and has various stops where walks or picnics by the water can be taken. Llanuwchllyn is also well known for its cultural associations with the Welsh language movement.

Spreading up from the eastern banks of the lake is **Penllyn Forest** which can be reached and passed through via **Cwm Hirnant** on an unclassified road. There is a picnic spot marked by the roadside and pleasant walks can be made from here. The road itself weaves through the forest to moorland, eventually continuing to **Llyn Efyrnwy** (**Lake Vyrnwy**).

The lakeside road passes through **Llandderfel**, whose 15th-century church has wooden relics that are worthy of a visit. A headless animal and pole, known as **St Derfel's Horse and Staff**, are thought to be the remnants of the figure of a saint on horseback which was sent to London to be put in the fire that burnt Friar Forest, Catherine of Aragon's confessor, in 1538.

2 South Snowdonia

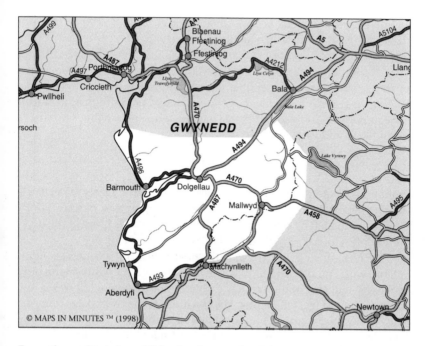

From the earliest days, Wales has been mined for its minerals. Gold was known here in prehistoric times and it was the Romans who started to mine the mineral seriously. Found in the Cambrian rocks in this southern area of Snowdonia, the Dolgellau gold belt stretches from Bontddu along the line of the River Mawddach. The modern gold rushes, which were both feverish and short-lived, date back no further than the mid 19th century and these sporadic bursts of enthusiasm continue, in a less manic fashion, today. Although, at their peak, there were mines that made great fortunes, the expense of locating the gold and extracting it are still prohibitive.

Gold has a way of turning the mind as no other mineral can but this area of Wales is also rich in other minerals. Copper, lead, and slate were also mined right up to the start of the 20th century and the scars that these industries left are plain to see today. Another lasting feature of these extraction processes are the numerous, now conserved, steam railway lines that were built to carry the minerals to the coast for shipment. There can be no greater way to view the countryside than from trains pulled by a steam engine and, in Wales particularly, the lines travel through some glorious countryside.

The railway lines of the mid to late 19th century were also responsible for changing the character of the coastline. Small fishing villages and sea ports became desirable holiday locations as the fashion for taking the sea air and health in general became an abiding Victorian pastime. Much of the Victorian and Edwardian architecture is still to be seen in many of the resorts that dot this part of the coastline.

The southern gateway to the Snowdonia National Park is dominated by the massive bulk of Cader Idris, a mountain which sweeps down to the sea to give a most spectacular coastline. Though not as high as its northern counterpart, Snowdon, this area has much to offer anyone who enjoys magnificent and varied countryside.

DOLGELLAU

Pronounced Dol-getl-aye and meaning Meadow of the Hazels, Dolgellau is the chief centre and market town for this southern area of Snowdonia. Pleasantly situated by the River Wnion, with Cader Idris rising in the background, the town is very Welsh in both custom and language.

Owain Glyndwr held a Welsh parliament here in 1404, later signing an alliance with France's Charles VI. Now, the town's narrow streets can only evoke those distant times but few early buildings remain. However, the seven arched bridge, which links the town across the river, dates from the early 17th century and, before the building of much of Dolgellau, to lure Victorian holidaymakers to the delights of Cader Idris, the town had, in the 17th century been a small, rural Quaker community. In the summer the town is a popular tourist spot, as well as being a junction to several main roads, so visitors must be prepared for the occasional bottleneck.

Cader Idris rises to some 2,927 feet southwest of Dolgellau and there are several routes to its summit. Meaning 'Chair of Idris', the mountain is named, according to tradition, after a great warrior and poet. It has a national nature reserve which interests botanists because of the alpine plants that prosper there. Cader Idris is now almost as popular as Snowdon in terms of visitors trekking to its summit. On a clear day, the Isle of Man and the Irish coast as well as views of the Mawddach Estuary and railway bridge can be seen.

Found in the heart of the town, **The Lion Milk Bar** was once one of the many National milk bars that could be found around Britain and, today, it is still a warm and friendly café owned and personally run by sisters, Elizabeth Jones and Paula Lloyd. Since taking over the premises at the beginning of the 1998 season, the sisters have, once again, put The

The Lion Milk Bar, Lion Street, Dolgellau, Gwynedd LL40 1DG Tel: 01341 423040

Lion Milk Bar on the map. A popular place, well recommended by the people of Dolgellau and the surrounding area, this café is open every day, except winter Sundays, to serve customers a delicious range of tasty snacks and meals. The ideal place for all the family, this spacious, comfortably furnished café caters for all tastes. As well as the special children's menu, the main menu is supplemented by a list of daily specials and there is always a mouth-watering array of home-made cakes to tempt everyone. For those who are unable to take advantage of the hospitality here, a take away service is also provided.

The Cross Foxes Inn, just to the east of Dolgellau, is a solid stone built late Victorian listed building that has been owned and personally run by Anelma and Iori Williams since the early 1980s. Built on the site of an old coaching inn and standing on what was a drovers' route, from here can be

The Cross Foxes Inn, Cross Foxes, Dolgellau, Gwynedd LL40 2SG Tel: 01341 422487

seen Cader Idris, Wales' third highest mountain, and the Arran mountain range. This is the perfect setting for the warm and friendly hospitality offered by the couple and, not only can customers find excellent food and drink here but there are also four spacious guest rooms that are available all year round.

Cosy and comfortable inside, The Cross Foxes Inn has several open fireplaces that are lit on cold nights and which are also home to Anelma's display of shiny brassware. Adding a homely touch, Anelma has also placed her pottery collection on shelves around the pub's walls. Here not only do the locals collect for a pint or two of fine ale but the inn is also well known for the delicious menu that is served at both lunchtime and in the evening. All in all, The Cross Foxes Inn offers all its customers the very best in food, drink, and accommodation.

Found just to the east of Dolgellau, in the village of **Tabor**, and over-looking the magnificent Mawddach estuary, **Fronoleu Farm Hotel** lies in a secluded position that makes it the ideal place for a relaxing holiday. Converted from an old 17th-century farmhouse, the hotel is owned and personally run by Maggie and Dewi Jones. Since arriving here in the 1980s, the couple have extended and completely refurbished the property, which was part of a Quaker settlement, and, today, this attractive hotel offers guests comfortable accommodation in a choice of 12 en-suite, stylish rooms. Care has been taken to retain many of the building's farmhouse features and the traditional character of the place combines well with the addition

Fronoleu Farm Hotel, Tabor, near Dolgellau, Gwynedd LL40 2PS
Tel: 01341 422361

of modern facilities to provide a unique farmhouse atmosphere. Dewi is the chef of the partnership and, as well as a substantial breakfast to set guests up for a day exploring the surroundings, the hotel's restaurant, which is also open to non-residents, offers an extensive menu of local and international dishes that are all freshly prepared and beautifully presented. The bar, too, is popular locally and, at weekends, a Welsh harpist adds to the traditional atmosphere created by the setting. With such glorious countryside right on its doorstep, guests will not be surprised to learn that this is a popular venue, locally, for wedding receptions and, once found, many visitors return time and time again.

NORTH OF DOLGELLAU

LLANFACHRAETH   MAP 3 REF G6
3 miles N of Dolgellau off A470

This charmingly situated village is an excellent place to visit for those who enjoy panoramic views as from here starts the three and a half mile **Precipice Walk** around the foot of **Foel Cynwch**. Good footwear is recommended for this quite rugged route which can be started from the National Park Car Park, on the country road just south of Llanfachraeth.

The village itself is home to the **Glasdir Arboretum** and it is also overlooked by Moel Offrwm, at the summit of which is an Iron Age fort. Also close by is **Nannau Hall** the ancient seat of the Vaughan family who owned much land in this area. It is said that an earlier house on the site belonged to Howel Sele, a cousin of Owain Glyndwr, who during a dispute with Glyndwr over Sele's Lancastrian sympathies, shot at but missed his cousin whilst out hunting. Glyndwr killed Sele whilst in a rage, then hid his body in a hollow oak, which later received a mention in Sir Walter Scott's *Marmion* as 'the spirit's blasted tree'. The old houses and cottages of the Nannau estate can easily be picked out by their decorated chimneys.

Found in this tiny hamlet, surrounded by luscious pastureland, woods, and Moel Offrwm (the Hill of Sacrifice) and close to the famous Precipice Walk, **Ty Isaf Farmhouse** is the perfect retreat from the hurly burly of late 20th century living. Up until 1985, the house stood at the centre of a working farm but, today, this charming house is the home of Raymond and Lorna Gear who know the area well, as Lorna's family originate from the village. Dating back to 1624, Ty Isaf is surrounded by a lovely large garden, edged by a rushing mountain stream. With three comfortable, en-suite guest rooms let on a bed and breakfast basis, this is the ideal place for a peaceful, tranquil holiday in the heart of glorious countryside. As well as the three guest rooms, each of which is named after the farm store rooms they once were, there is also a guests' lounge with television and

Ty Isaf Farmhouse, Llanfachraeth, near Dolgellau
Gwynedd LL40 2EA Tel: 01341 423261

video and a separate residents' reading room with many books to inspire the heart. Breakfast and the evening meal (available by prior arrange-ment) are served in the dining room which, like the rest of the house, is a cosy and comfortable room that reflects the age of the property with its exposed beams and stylish furniture. The perfect place for a break away from the rigours of life, guests should also look out for Lorna's two pet llamas, Math and Mathonwy, who are named after the Mabinogion's Celtic legend!

GANLLWYD   Map 3 ref F6
4 miles N of Dolgellau on A470

This hamlet gives its name to the attractive valley in which it is found and which is, in turn, surrounded by the 16,000 acre **Coed-y-Brenin Forest**. Now chiefly an area of conifers, there were once vast expanses of broad-leaved woodland here, some of which still survives at the National Trust owned Dolmelynllyn estate. In the heart of the forest can be found a series of hundreds of steps, known as the **Roman Steps**, which though certainly not Roman, climb up through the rocks and heather of the Rhinog Mountains. They are thought to have been part of a late medieval trade route between the coastal region around Harlech and England.

Ganllwyd, a good stopping off point to visit the waterfall **Rhaiadr Du** (Black Waterfall), was once a centre for gold mining and, during the 1880s, the nearby mine at Gwynfynydd was prosperous enough to attract some 250 miners. The mine had produced in the region of 40,000 ounces of gold by the time it closed in 1917.

To the north of the village is **Pont Dolgefeiliau** (The Field of Smiths) across the River Eden, that is so called as drovers used to prepare their cattle here before setting off to London.

LLANFAIR
MAP 3 REF F6
11 miles NW of Dolgellau on A496

Between 1853 and 1906, Llanfair was a prosperous slate mining village and the old, deep quarries, the **Chwarel Hên Llanfair Slate Caverns**, are now open to the public. A trip here provides a fascinating insight into this once important local industry and the guided tours around the old work-

ings take visitors through the main tunnel and into the Crypt and the Cathedral Cavern. The descent of Jacob's Ladder leads to tunnels and chambers where drill holes for blasting can still be seen and the image of a human face is visible in the rock in one of the caverns. The slate within this mine lies at a 30 degree angle from horizontal which, considering it was extracted from these huge

Chwarel Hên Llanfair Slate Caverns, Llanfair

caverns by candlelight, highlights the terrible working conditions the miners endured. The temperature, which seldom exceeds 50 degrees Fahrenheit, emphasises the harsh conditions and, however warm it is on the surface, it is wise to bear this in mind.

LLANBEDR
MAP 3 REF F6
10 miles NW of Dolgellau on A496

This village is an excellent starting point for walks along the lovely valleys of Rivers Artro and Nant-col and into the Rhinog mountains. At 2,360 feet **Rhinog Fawr** may not be the highest local peak but, from its summit, there are superb views over the Coed-y-Brenin Forest to the Eden valley. On the route up the River Artro is a hut circle and slightly away from the river are stone circles originating from the Iron Age. There is also a Farm Trail, which goes on to explain the workings of a Welsh hill farm, and a

Nature Trail to follow before the path climbs beyond Llyn Cwmbychan and into woodland.

Those not so keen on walking may be interested in **Maes Artro Village**, which is now an award winning tourist attraction but once the living quarters for pilots of Fighter Squadrons during the Second World War. Today, it houses an **RAF Museum**, aquarium, Village of Yesteryear, craft shops and many other attractions as well as a gift shop and café. The RAF still maintains a base close by which is passed on the way to Shell Island.

SHELL ISLAND   MAP 3 REF E6
12 miles NW of Dolgellau off A496

More correctly described as a peninsula which is cut off at high tide (beware, however, the tide comes in with surprising speed!), Shell Island is a treasure trove of seashells and wildlife. The shoreline, a mixture of pebble beaches with rock pools and golden sands, is ideal for children to explore and uncover some of the over 100 varieties of shells that have been found there. Seals are often seen close by and there is plenty of birdlife; surprising considering the fairly regular taking off and land of training aircraft from the base nearby.

DYFFRYN ARDUDWY   MAP 3 REF F6
9 miles W of Dolgellau on A496

Neolithic remains, as well as the remnants of Iron and Bronze Ages settlements, abound in this area and in the village, just behind the school, are two such burial chambers. Perhaps the most interesting is **Arthur's Quoit**, a chamber the capstone of which is said to have been thrown from the summit of Moelfre by King Arthur.

Surrounded by open farmland and with glorious views over Cardigan Bay on one side and Snowdonia National Park on the other, **Cadwgan Hotel** can certainly be said to offer something for everyone. This large house was built at the turn of the century and has been, in its time, a convalescent home and a farmhouse. Today, it is owned by Mervyn and Jane Lewis who, since they bought the premises in the early 1980s, have made it one of the most popular hotels along this stretch of coast. As well as the three en-suite guest rooms, there are two recently created self-catering apartments, and also, during the high season, a caravan for hire in the hotel's extensive grounds.

As well as the excellent accommodation, Cadwgan Hotel's popular dining room is open to both residents and non-residents for lunch and dinner and the bar, too, is a well frequented local meeting place. The hotel's facilities are matched by the large and well maintained garden, with safe children's play area and delightful patio and seating, the games room, the

Cadwgan Hotel, Dyffryn Ardudwy, Gwynedd LL44 2HA
Tel: 01341 247240

friendly atmosphere, and the excellent hospitality. This is a superb place
to stay and guests should remember to book their table in the non-smoking dining room.

Surrounded by some wonderful countryside, **Byrdir** is a typical Welsh
hill farm that has been owned and run by Anne and Ifan Jones since the
late 1970s. As well as the herd of Welsh black cows and Charolais bull, the
couple also have a flock of Welsh mountain sheep and though they do
most of the work themselves they are helped by their sheep dogs, Bych
and Fflei. This work obviously keeps the couple busy but they also have
time to offer excellent bed and breakfast accommodation from their delightful stone built farmhouse. Though modernised, this charming home

Byrdir, Dyffryn Ardudwy, Gwynedd LL44 2EA
Tel: 01341 247200 Fax: 01341 247889

has retained many of its original features, including the wooden beams and there is a wonderful inglenook fireplace in the lounge.

As well as the en-suite guest rooms in the main house, as some old farm buildings became redundant, Anne and Ifan have undertaken an extensive refurbishment programme and they are now able to offer outstanding accommodation in these cottage bedrooms as well. Beautifully converted, these rooms, like the rest of the house provide a quiet haven for a peaceful and relaxing holiday with charming and thoughtful hosts who work to ensure that everyone makes the most of their stay. Children, but not pets, are welcome to the Byrdir and, when their farming commitments allow, Anne and Ifan are happy to take guests on a farm trail, with perhaps some hands on farming thrown in!

Amidst beautiful countryside and close to the village of Dyffryn Ardudwy, lies **Ystumgwern Farm**, the home of John and Jane Williams. John's family has been farming the land here for many years and today the couple, whilst still working the farm, offer visitors to the area excellent bed and breakfast accommodation in a range of luxury apartments which open out onto a delightful flower filled courtyard. These superb apartments have been created in a traditional stone barn in a sympathetic and

Ystumgwern Farm, Dyffryn Ardudwy, Gwynedd LL44 2DD Tel: 01341 247249 Fax: 01341 247171

imaginative fashion and provide comfortable accommodation for up to four people whilst retaining much of the original building's character. Furnished and decorated to the very highest standards, each of the apartments has a modern kitchen fitted with the latest equipment as well as a comfortable living room with dining area. The bedrooms, also stylishly furnished, are the perfect place for a tranquil and peaceful night's rest and have en-suite bathrooms. With cosy apartments for romantic couples to those with two bedrooms, the accommodation here is exceptional as well as being flexible enough for a family. Breakfast is taken in the traditional 16th century farmhouse where with considerable style John and Jane have created a luxurious homely atmosphere.

Set in amidst some of Wales' most glorious countryside lies **Ynys**, which offers visitors a range of superb self-catering accommodation that is not only close to the sandy beaches of the Cambrian coastline but also surrounded by acres of fertile farmland. The creation of John and Jane Williams these luxury apartments, which vary in size from cosy flats for romantic couples to large apartments for all the family, are all found within a charming old barn. The sensitive conversion to provide modern facilities without loss of this splendid building's character has been imaginatively achieved and, along with the exceptional attention to detail, many features, such as the thick stone walls and large oak beams, have been retained.

Ynys, Ystumgwern Farm, Dyffryn Ardudwy, Gwynedd LL44 2DD
Tel: 01341 247249 Fax: 01341 247171

Furnished and decorated to the very highest standards, each apartment has a stylish and comfortable living room, with dining area, and an up to the minute kitchen that is spotlessly clean and fitted with all the latest equipment. The charming bedrooms again meet the high standards of the rest of the apartments and each has an en-suite bathroom. Outside these five luxury apartments is a delightful flower filled courtyard, a specially constructed play area for the children, and a games room with table tennis and darts.

This, however, is not all Ynys has to offer the holidaymaker as John and Jane have two large and attractive cottages. Found down their own private lane, the refurbishment of this traditional 14th century farmhouse, once the home of the Lord of Gwytheyrn, into these two cottages has been undertaken in the same excellent manner as the apartments. The larger of the cottages, which can sleep eight, has a ground floor en-suite bedroom that has been carefully planned for the wheelchair user as well as three further first floor bedrooms and two bathrooms. The smaller, with three delightful bedrooms and two bathrooms, is, like its neighbour, a warm and welcoming place for a family holiday and has not only a superbly styled modern kitchen with dining area but also a comfortable living room with an open fireplace. Each cottage also has its own private garden complete with outdoor furniture and a separate barbecue area.

TAL-Y-BONT   Map 3 ref F6
8 miles W of Dolgellau on A496

This village is the home of the **Old Country Life Centre** which as well as covering early farming methods used in the area also has exhibits on local shipwrecks. This too is a delightful place from which to take pleasant walks from the coast and up into the surrounding hills.

Anyone hoping to find a more perfect position for a caravan park will have to look a long way before they find somewhere better than **Sarnfaen Holiday Park**. Just yards from the beach and with a backdrop of craggy mountains, this really is a superb place for a family holiday. Owned and personally run by Caroline Pritchard and Robert Gallimore, there is a great range of choice of holiday home, from two berth caravans to those sleeping seven, and, as well as being beautifully kept and maintained, the layout

Sarnfaen Holiday Park, Tal-y-bont, near Barmouth
Gwynedd LL43 2AQ   Tel & Fax: 01341 247241
E-mail: robert.gallimore@sarnfaen.force9.net

of the park has been carefully planned and landscaped to ensure that privacy is guaranteed. The ideal place for children, the parks numerous facilities include an indoor heated swimming pool, a children's play area, a games room, a shop, a coffee shop, and a dog walking area. Caroline and Robert, a charming couple with two young daughters of their own, know how important the small details are during a family holiday and they are on hand and willing to help, whether it is providing garden chairs or information on the wide variety of things to do in the surrounding area.

LLANELLTYD   MAP 3 REF F6
1 mile N of Dolgellau on A470

This is the point at which the Rivers Wen and Wnion, boosted by other

Cymmer Abbey

water further upland, meet to form the Mawddach Estuary. Close by, just across the River Wen, lie the ruins of the 12th-century **Cymmer Abbey**, which was one of the two Cistercian abbeys in the Snowdonia region during the Middle Ages. (The other abbey being Conwy Abbey founded in 1172.) Founded in 1199 by Cistercian monks, Cymmer was granted a charter in 1209 and held a substantial estate in the area. Now only parts of the church, refectory, and chapter house remain in this very attractive setting.

WEST OF DOLGELLAU

PENMAEN   MAP 3 REF F7
2 miles W of Dolgellau on A493

Close to the village and overlooking the estuary of the River Mawddach is the RSPB **Nature Reserve - Mawddach Valley**. As well as the great wealth of bird and wildlife seen on the reserve, the Nature Information Centre, housed in an old railway signal box, is full of interesting information and helpful advice to those wishing to find out more about the creatures who have made the reserve their home.

BONTDDU   MAP 3 REF F7

5 miles W of Dolgellau on A496

Looking at this pleasant and agreeable village it is hard to imagine that it was, over 100 years ago, a bustling centre of Welsh gold mining industry. Apparently there were 24 mines operating in the area around the village, one of them providing gold for the Royal wedding rings. However, since the mines workings have ceased, only the occasional fragment has been found.

BARMOUTH   MAP 3 REF F7

6 miles W of Dolgellau on A496

Occupying an picturesque location by the mouth of the River Mawddach, Barmouth was once a small port with an equally small shipbuilding industry. As the fashion for invalids seeking out sea air grew rapidly in the 18th century, the character of Barmouth changed to accommodate those flocking here for the bracing air. Those suffering from scurvy were even fed seaweed, which is rich in Vitamin C, that grew in abundance in the estuary. However, the Barmouth seen today is, like many seaside resorts, a product of the railway age and the Victorian architecture is still very apparent.

Built over 125 years ago and half a mile in length, the railway viaduct which spans the estuary, not only carries trains but there is also a walkway on the bridge from which there are magnificent views of the town, coast, and estuary.

Close by is **Ty Gywn**, a 15th-century house said to have been built for Henry Tudor, Earl of Richmond (later Henry VII) and which was used as the meeting place whilst he plotted to overthrow Richard III. It now contains an exhibition on Tudor times along with maritime artifacts. Barmouth is also home to an **RNLI Museum**.

The town's harbour, which hosts a regatta, is overlooked by **Dinas Oleu**, a National Trust property and the starting point of the pleasant **Panoramic Walk** where views across the estuary are worth the walk alone. The first property given to the newly formed National Trust in 1895, the land was a gift from the local wealthy philanthropist, Mrs Fanny Talbot, a friend of two of the Trust's founding members.

LLANABER   MAP 3 REF F7

7 miles W of Dolgellau on A496

Found close to the clifftops, the village church (once the parish church of Barmouth) is said to have been used by smugglers who hid their spoils inside the tombs in the churchyard. Dating from the 10th century this place of worship has, amongst other things, an interesting doorway claimed to be one of the best examples of early English architecture. The village now reaches down almost to the popular resort of Barmouth.

Situated in the village and just a mile or so from Barmouth, **Llwyndu Farmhouse**, the home of Paula and Peter Thompson, occupies a splendid position overlooking Cardigan Bay. Probably dating back to the late 16th and early 17th century, this wonderful farmhouse retains many of its original features, including oak beamed ceilings, stone walls, mullioned windows, and inglenook fireplaces but, perhaps, the finest feature of all is the circular stone staircase. In the time that Peter and Paula have lived here they have slowly refurbished the house and, today, it is a stylish and relaxing home with an informal atmosphere that is much appreciated by those lucky enough to be staying here.

There are three guest rooms, as well as four rooms in a converted barn, all as carefully furnished and decorated as the rest of the house, and there are also some very unique added attractions. The standard of hospitality offered by Peter and Paula would put many four and five star hotels to shame and those looking for good food and wine need look no further. The restaurant, which is open to non-residents, has an enviable and well deserved reputation locally and, though modern in style, has, at its heart, the traditional values of quality, fresh ingredients and a balanced association of flavours. Guests at Llwyndu Farmhouse will also be sampling equally

Llwyndu Farmhouse, Llanaber, near Barmouth, Gwynedd LL42 1RR
Tel: 01341 280144 Fax: 01341 281236

delicious breakfasts in the morning and, on Sundays, when the restaurant is closed, Peter and Paula are happy to recommend several alternative eating places. The house has a long and well documented history and back as far as the 16th century was noted for its hospitality, song, and good ale - the tradition continues.

SOUTH OF DOLGELLAU

TAL-Y-LLYN   MAP 3 REF F7
5 miles S of Dolgellau on B4405

This tiny hamlet lies at the southwestern end of the **Tal-y-llyn Lake**, above which lies the Tal-y-llyn Pass, and both are overshadowed by the crags of Cader Idris to the north. A great place for trout fishermen, the village is also home to a simple early 17th-century church that has an unusual chancel ceiling of square panels that are decorated with carved roses.

Overlooking Tal-y-llyn Lake, **Dolffanog Fach** is a beautiful country guest house as well as being the home of Meirwen and John Pughe who farm the surrounding land with Welsh Mountain sheep and cattle. Dating from 1770, this lovely old building is as stylish and full of character inside as its exterior would suggest. Guests take their meals in a traditional beamed room that has a Welsh slate floor and the cosy residents' lounge features

Dolffanog Fach, Tal-y-llyn, near Tywyn, Gwynedd LL36 9AJ
Tel & Fax: 01654 761235

an inglenook fireplace with a wood-burning stove. On display in the lounge are also the results of John's hobby, carpentry, and the spinning wheel and horses and carts are both interesting and skilfully made. The family's talents do not end there by any means as the home-cooked breakfast and optional evening meal are both of an equally high standard.

An ideal location for those interested in hill walking, ornithology, and fishing, the three en-suite guest rooms are as well furnished and as comfortable as the rest of the house and are sure to provide guests with a relaxing night's sleep. This is a superb place to stay for all the family as, in a separate building in the couple's lovely garden, there is a games room that is sure to keep everyone amused.

LLANFIHANGEL-Y-PENNANT   MAP 3 REF F7
6 miles S of Dolgellau off B4405

Close by this small hamlet lie the ruins of **Mary Jones's Cottage**. After saving six years for a Welsh bible in the early 1800s Mary Jones, the daughter of a weaver, walked to Bala to purchase a copy from Thomas Charles. Thomas had no copies of the Good Book available for sale so he gave her his own copy and the episode inspired the founding of the British and Foreign Bible Society. Mary lived to the ripe old age of 88 and was buried at Bryn-crug, while her bible is preserved in the Society's headquarters in London.

To the southwest of Llanfihangel-y-pennant lie the ruins of **Castell-y-Bere**, a hill top fortress started by Llewelyn the Great in 1223. Taken by the Earl of Pembrokeshire on behalf of Edward I in 1283, it stayed in English hands for two years until retaken and razed to the ground by the Welsh. Although Edward hoped to create a borough here it never developed after being recaptured by the Welsh.

A little further south, in the former slate quarry village of **Abergynolwyn**, is a **Museum** dedicated to the story of slate and the industry that dominated this area at one time.

CORRIS   MAP 3 REF G7
6 miles S of Dolgellau on A487

The **Railway Museum** in the village recalls the days of slate in the area and the railway which, though dismantled in 1948, provided the Tal-y-llyn Railway with engines. From the Forest Enterprise picnic site between the village and **Aberllefenni** a marked trail takes in some of the now disused quarry buildings.

Also in the village, at the Craft Centre, is the fascinating **King Arthur's Labyrinth**. This maze of underground tunnels and caverns are explored on a guided boat trip and on foot when the tales of King Arthur and other legends are uncovered. **Corris Craft Centre**, home to a variety of working craftsmen and women, is an excellent place to find an unusual and unique gift and, for those in need of refreshment, there is a café serving all manner of home-made goodies.

Just to the south of the village is the **Centre for Alternative Technology**, an independent educational charity which makes an interesting and informative visit. At the centre wind turbines, solar energy, and water power can be seen being put to use for the benefit of the community that live in its grounds. The centre's shop sells green products and the café serves a wide variety of vegetarian dishes.

MALLWYD   MAP 3 REF G7
9 miles SE of Dolgellau on A470

The **Brigand Inn**, in this small village, recalls the days during the 16th century when the area was menaced by a gang known as the 'Red Robbers of Mawddwy'. Eighty gang members were executed in 1554 and the survivors exacted some revenge by murdering their prosecutor Baron Lewis Owen at nearby **Llidiart-y-Barwn**.

DINAS MAWDDWY   MAP 3 REF G7
8 miles SE of Dolgellau on A470

A quiet village today, in the Middle Ages, Dinas Mawddwy was a centre of local power but, unfortunately, the only surviving feature from those days is the rather overgrown pack horse bridge, **Pont Minllyn**. A gateway to the upper Dyfi valley and the Aran range, this once rural village, whose economy centred around farming and forestry, was once also alive with quarries and mines. At the old village railway station, which lay on the line to Machynlleth, not only can visitors see cloth being woven in the traditional fashion at **Meirion Mill** but there is a visitor centre, craft shop, and café too.

A couple of miles north of Dinas Mawddwy and with lovely, uninterrupted views of the Cowarch valley, lies **Bryncelyn Farm**, the home of Eldrydd Edwards and her family. Immediately surrounded by their own 750 acres of farmland, where they raise sheep and suckling cows, the Edwards family has been here since the late 1960s. For most of this time they have also been offering some of the best bed and breakfast accommodation in this area. Not only is this one of the most idyllic settings but the two en-suite guest rooms offer levels of comfort and peace and quiet that no London five star hotel could possibly match. As well as breakfast, delicious home-cooked evening meals can be prepared by prior arrangement. However, for those who prefer to take care of themselves, just a short walk

Bryncelyn Farm, Dinas Mawddwy, Powys SY20 9JG
Tel: 01650 531289

away but with equally magnificent views, the Edwards family also have a charming refurbished cottage available for self-catering holidays. Sleeping up to seven people this is ideal for larger families and groups.

ABERDYFI

Also commonly known by its English name, Aberdovey, this now quiet resort at the mouth of the River Dyfi was once one of the most important ports along the Welsh Coast. Shipbuilding flourished here alongside the busy port which was recorded, on one particular occasion, as having 180 ships unloading or waiting for a berth. However, the **Outward Bound Sea School** and its **Museum** ensures that Aberdyfi's relationship with the sea continues.

The town has been attracting holidaymakers since Edwardian times, when the railways made such trips possible for many more people, and this is reflected in much of the town's architecture.

Overlooking the beach, in the centre of Aberdyfi **The Bear of Amsterdam Café** is a charming family run establishment that takes its name from a Spanish galleon that once visited the town. Owned and personally run by Anna and George Smith, with the help of their daughter Gretta, this attractive and comfortably furnished café is full of character as befits a 200-year-old building. Open every day during the season from 10.00 to 20.30, but with shorter hours during the winter, The Bear of Amsterdam serves a full and comprehensive menu of tasty snacks and meals.

George is the chef of the team and he was, for many years, head chef at one of the nearby top class hotels, so customers can expect to be treated to a freshly prepared meal that is also well presented. Though not licensed, diners are very welcome to bring their own wine, for which no corkage

The Bear of Amsterdam Café, 9 Sea View Terrace, Aberdyfi
Gwynedd LL35 0LW Tel: 01654 767684

charge is made. This is a popular café, well known locally, and highly regarded for the superb fresh fish that they serve on Friday evenings.

Just a few yards from the sea and sands, **The Grapevine Restaurant** is the place to come to for fine food and drink and excellent hospitality in delightful surroundings. Housed in a building dating from the mid 1800s, this was originally three cottages which became the Temperance Hotel in the late 19th century. Today, this charming restaurant is owned and personally run by Julie and William Moeran who have created an interior full of character and warmth. Using antique oak taken from a barn in Shropshire, the exposed wall and ceiling beams and heavy oak doors perfectly reflect the age of the building and provide an intimate setting for a delicious meal. Open every day from Easter to Halloween and with limited opening during the winter, the imaginative menu of interesting, freshly prepared dishes is varied and combines flavours from around the world

**The Grapevine Restaurant, 1 Chapel Square, Aberdyfi
Gwynedd LL35 0EL Tel: 01654 767448**

with the very best of local produce. A popular place locally, this friendly, relaxed restaurant is certainly a place worthy of a visit.

NORTH OF ABERDYFI

PENNAL   MAP 3 REF F8
6 miles NE of Aberdyfi on A493

This small village clustered around its bridge, at the head of the charmingly named Happy Valley, was once the site of a Roman fort and it was also the home of one of Owain Glyndwr's Welsh parliaments.

TYWYN   MAP 3 REF F8
3 miles N of Aberdyfi on A493

This coastal town and seaside resort on Cardigan Bay has long sandy beaches, dunes, a promenade, and it is also the start (or finish) of the famous **Tal-y-llyn Railway**. First used in 1865 to transport slate down from the Brynglas Quarry to Tywyn where it fed the mainline railway, the narrow gauge Great Little Train was soon carrying passengers and has the longest continuous services of any railway in Wales. After the closure of the quarry in 1947 the Tal-y-llyn Railway Preservation Society took control. The railway stops at several places, allowing the passenger the opportunity to walk in the surrounding country and the round journey to Nant Gwernol Station and back takes about two hours. At the station here is a **Narrow Gauge Railway Museum** and shop to browse around.

Also worthy of a visit is **St Cadfan's Church** home of the famous **St Cadfan Stone** inscribed in, what is believed to be, the earliest example of written Welsh and which is estimated to date from the 7th century.

Found in the heart of this popular resort, **The Tredegar Arms**, known locally as The Tred, dates from the 19th century and its old stables can still be seen behind the pub. Catering for all ages, this well frequented and highly regarded inn has been personally run by Toni and Spike Bryan since 1994 and it is very much due to them that The Tredegar Arms has such an enviable reputation within the local area.

The Tredegar Arms, 10 College Green, Tywyn, Gwynedd LL36 9BS
Tel: 01654 710368 Fax: 01654 712510

As well as serving an excellent range of ales, beers, and lagers, it is the delicious and extensive menus of imaginative and creative dishes that have really put the pub on the map. Either served in the pub's restaurant or in the bar area, there is sure to be something to suit every occasion, whether it be a quick and tasty bite or a celebration meal. Spike is the chef of the partnership and the truly international nature of the dishes, with everything from haggis to crocodile on the list, certainly makes dining here an exciting safari tour. Add to this the live music on Tuesday evenings, the cosy surroundings and unusual decorations, and the small patio beer garden and The Tredegar Arms really is a fine example of the perfect pub.

LLANEGRYN
6 miles N of Aberdyfi off A493

MAP 3 REF F7

The lovely church in this quiet village has one of the finest rood screens in Wales and it is thought to have come from Cymmer Abbey after the Reformation. From the village the road travels up the Dysynni valley and passes the famous outcrop **Craig y Aderyn (Bird Rock)**. Although five miles from the sea, which once lapped at its feet, this outcrop is still a breeding ground for cormorants.

The home of Anne and David Sylvester since 1991, **Cefn Coch Country Guest House** is a charming former coaching inn that dates back to 1867. Set in its own private gardens and with extensive views over the surrounding glorious countryside, not only do the couple offer excellent bed and breakfast accommodation from this delightful home but they also have charming tea rooms. The accommodation at Cefn Coch comprises five comfortable and cosy guest rooms which, like the rest of the house, are stylishly decorated and furnished, as well as a residents' lounge

Cefn Coch Country Guest House, Llanegryn, near Tywyn
Gwynedd LL36 9SD Tel & Fax: 01654 712193

with shelves of books and videos to enjoy. A real home-cooked breakfast is included and both packed lunches and an evening meal are available by prior arrangement. The accommodation here is not suitable for children or smokers.

The separate tea rooms, which are open every day in the season and from Friday to Sunday for the rest of the year, offer a tasty menu of light meals and snacks as well as some mouth-watering, home-made cakes. For fine weather there is plenty of outdoor seating from which the splendid surrounding countryside can be seen.

Found overlooking the beautiful Dysynni Valley, just south of Llanegryn in the village of **Bryn-crug**, and only a couple of miles from Tywyn, **Tynllwyn Caravan and Camping Park** is an ideal place for those who enjoy glorious countryside, birdwatching, and picturesque walks. Open from March to the end of October, the park, which has been owned and personally run by Pat and Pam McEvoy since 1988, is well laid out and maintained, in a lovely country setting.

With room for 18 touring caravans and 50 tents, the park also has six static luxury caravans for hire that offer all the latest amenities and comforts. Very much a family site, Tynllwyn not only has a laundry, an ablutions block, and a small provisions shop but there is also a safe children's play area and a pets' corner. The family pet is also welcome by prior arrangement but no single sex groups are permitted on the site. Well placed for all the places of interest in the surrounding area, the Tal-y-llyn steam railway runs alongside the park and one of its stations is only 50 yards away along a quiet country lane.

Tynllwyn Caravan and Camping Park, Bryn-crug, near Tywyn, Gwynedd LL36 9RD Tel & Fax: 01654 710370

LLANGELYNNIN
Map 3 ref F7
7 miles N of Aberdyfi on A493

The **Ancient Church** above the sea at Llangelynnin dates from the 12th century and contains undated murals and a stoup that was said to have continually held water. The relatively modern, 19th-century pews are also interesting as they have names printed upon them.

FAIRBOURNE
Map 3 ref F7
10 miles N of Aberdyfi on A493

This growing holiday resort lies on the opposite side of the Mawddach Estuary from Barmouth. The beach stretches for about two miles and the **Fairbourne Railway** runs to the ferry which carries passengers across the water to Barmouth. With a gauge of only 15 inches, this is the smallest railway in Wales and it began life in the 19th century as a horse drawn tramway before changing to steam in 1916. It was saved from extinction by enthusiasts after falling into disuse and it is now a popular attraction for visitors.

ARTHOG
Map 3 ref F7
11 miles N of Aberdyfi on A493

Overlooking the Mawddach Estuary, this elongated village is a starting point for walks into Cader Idris. Beginning with a sheltered woodland path, the trail climbs up to the two Cregennen lakes (both owned by the National Trust) from which there are glorious mountain views.

Found just outside Fairbourne and with splendid views of the Mawddach Estuary, **Bwlch Gwyn Farm** is owned by John and Gemma Evans. From

Bwlch Gwyn Farm, Arthog, near Fairbourne, Gwynedd LL39 1BX
Tel: 01341 250107

this working farm, in 1957, John's father started the popular pony treks that take visitors on a choice of rides around the surrounding countryside. Aimed at competent riders, the hacks, which are available from March to October, take in much of the local scenery and offer visitors the opportunity to see the landscape in an interesting and exciting manner.   For beginners, there are riding lessons all year round.

Also from the farm, John and Gemma have a number of luxury caravans which they hire out on a self-catering basis for the season.   Quite and peaceful, this secluded site also has fine views over the estuary as it makes an ideal place from which to explore this interesting stretch of Welsh coast line.

3 Lleyn Peninsula

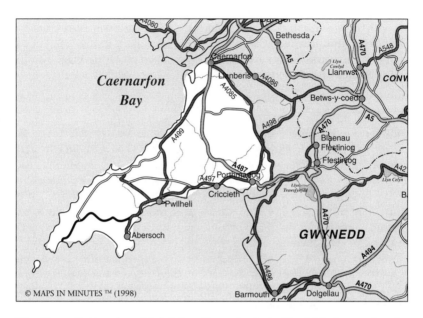

© MAPS IN MINUTES ™ (1998)

The Lleyn Peninsula, which takes its name from the Irish for peninsula, forms the northern boundary to the great curve of Cardigan Bay. It is also the most westerly area of Wales and, jutting out into the Irish Sea. Until the 5th century there was a significant Irish population in the region. Perhaps the most remote part of North Wales, this is a region where both the Welsh language and traditions are upheld.

In medieval times, the western most tip of the peninsula, Bardsey Island, was a place of great pilgrimage and the ancient route to Aberdaron, from where the pilgrims sailed to their destination, can still, in parts, be followed today. Not only are there still some reminders to the dedication of these long ago travellers to be found here but there are also numerous hill forts including the hut circle of Tre'r Ceiri.

Today, however, the Lleyn Peninsula is a delightful holiday location that draws people to its sandy beaches and wealth of water sports. Made fashionable in Victorian times, with the coming of the railways, these charming seaside resorts have remained small and not turned into the larger, somewhat brasher places that can be found elsewhere. The small villages of the peninsula are also charming and with many quiet, narrow lanes, there is much to explore off the beaten track. The childhood home of perhaps Wales' greatest politician, David Lloyd George, Llanystumdwy, whilst remembering its famous son, is still a perfect example of a small coastal village.

On the southeastern edge of the peninsula is an altogether different, but equally wonderful place, Portmeirion. Known to many who are familiar with the television series *The Prisoner*, the town is the delightful creation of the eccentric architect, Clough Williams-Ellis. Built in the 1920s in an Italian style, it was Williams-Ellis' dream to build an ideal village and its many annual visitors certainly agree.

PORTHMADOG

This busy town, where all the needs of residents and visitors are to be found, can be, particularly on rainy days, quite packed as holidaymakers take advantage of its many amenities which include a cinema, the **Porthmadog Pottery**, galleries as well as all manner of eating places. Out of the town towards Tremadog, across **The Cob**, the scenery to the left is quite magical and, at low tide, cattle graze alongside herons and other seabirds. The backdrop of the mountains puts in mind a Turner painting and at times the dilemma of concentrating on the narrow-walled road and the scenery can be difficult. The best way to appreciate the view is perhaps to walk along the embankment. At the far end a toll gate, manned by rather energetic individuals, requires a small fee which goes towards the upkeep of the embankment.

Today it is hard to believe that Porthmadog was once the busiest slate port in North Wales and, in fact, the town would never have existed if it had not been for William Maddocks. A Lincolnshire MP and a great entrepreneur, Maddocks, in the early 19th century, drained the mud flats that made up this estuary to create land for grazing cattle. The great embankment, built to keep the tides at bay, enclosed some 7,000 acres of land and the rerouted River Glaslyn soon produced a deep water channel that was ideal for the docks. Naming Porthmadog after himself (Tremadog to the west was named after his brother), the town began to flourish by the 1830s.

Though no longer a port, the history of the town and its waterfront is described in the **Maritime Museum** where, too, the importance of the trade in slate and Porthmadog's shipbuilding industry are told. The town is also home to one terminus of the **Welsh Highland Railway**, which in 1922, was the longest narrow gauge railway in Wales and now runs between Porthmadog and Caernarfon via Snowdonia. Closed to traffic in 1937, the line is only in operation today due to the hard work of a group of dedicated volunteers. As well as taking a memorable journey along the line, visitors can browse around the shop in the town and enjoy delicious, home-made refreshments at the café.

Found just off Porthmadog's main street, **Yr Hen Fecws** is a charming bistro and coffee house that is housed in a delightful 18th-century stone built terrace house. Owned and personally run by Helen and Michael since 1995, the bistro is well known and comes highly recommended by the people of Porthmadog and the surrounding area. Open every day in the summer and six days a week in the winter, Yr Hen Fecws, which means The Old Bakery, is certainly the place to come to for those who enjoy excellent, home-cooked food. Helen is the chef of the partnership and, be it lunchtime or in the evening, the menus are a delicious mix of traditional dishes and imaginative meals created by blending the best of local

Yr Hen Fecws, 15-16 Lombard Street, Porthmadog
Gwynedd LL49 9AP Tel: 01766 514625

produce with flavours from around the world. The addition of a mouthwatering blackboard of daily specials and desserts completes the appetising choice.

The surroundings too are imaginative, where warm and vibrant colours blend perfectly with the original exposed beams, stone fireplace and polished wooden floor of the building. Finally, Helen and Michael also offer comfortable bed and breakfast accommodation in the property adjoining the bistro as well as above. Furnished and decorated to the same high standard as the restaurant, this is an excellent place to stay and children are welcome both here and in the bistro.

The oldest public house in Porthmadog is **The Ship**, an attractive place built in 1824 as a harbour inn and easily recognisable by the model sailing ship perched on top of the entrance canopy. Managed by Nia and Robert Jones since 1985, the interior is beautifully decorated in a nautical theme and welcoming. In fact, The Ship is ideal for a family meal out since it offers an extensive, very reasonably priced menu that is sure to offer something for everyone. Nia and Gywnedd Williams are the chefs of the

**The Ship, Lombard Street, Porthmadog, Gwynedd LL49 9AP
Tel: 01766 512990**

establishment and, as well as the mouth-watering menu all prepared from fresh local produce, there is an ever changing list of daily specials from which to choose. The beer here also matches the same high standard of the cuisine and only feature real ales. Open all day, every day, The Ship is an ideal place for excellent food and drink.

The Rob Piercy Gallery, just of Porthmadog's High Street, is a moderately sized artist run gallery that is housed in an old converted warehouse. Over the 20 years that Rob Piercy has been painting professionally, his reputation as a painter of mountains has grown steadily and today he is one of Wales' premier landscape painters. Born in Porthmadog, Rob, a keen walker and climber from an early age, has been inspired by the often bleak landscape of northwest Wales and this has been a constant theme throughout his work, from his days at art school, through his teaching career, until he became a full time professional artist in 1989.

Rob, along with his wife Enid, bought the gallery premises in 1986, and, over a number of years they have gradually renovated and refurbished the building to create the gallery seen today. There are four key areas within the building: three of which are devoted to Rob's work whilst the fourth houses exhibitions of the work of other local artists. In addition to the original watercolours on display there is also an excellent range of high quality limited edition prints and cards that are taken from Rob's paintings. As a reminder of a holiday in North Wales, one of the Rob's pictures is sure to become a treasured possession.

The Rob Piercy Gallery, Snowdon Street, Porthmadog
Gwynedd LL49 9BT Tel & Fax: 01766 513833

Situated on a corner in the centre of the town, **Owens Hotel** is an attractive black and white building that is hard to miss. Built in 1864, this charming and delightful place has been owned and personally run since 1993 by Cathrin and John Bull. Open all year round, this ideally located hotel offers comfortable accommodation in a choice of ten guest rooms. Varying in size and with some en-suite, the rooms are all furnished and

**Owens Hotel, 71 High Street, Porthmadog, Gwynedd LL49 9EU
Tel: 01766 512098**

decorated to a high standard and provide the perfect place for a relaxing night's rest. Children and pets are both welcomed at this friendly establishment.

However, there is more to Owens Hotel than its comfortable guest rooms as, downstairs, is a popular restaurant that is open to non-residents. Highly regarded for its delicious menu, from snacks and light meals at lunchtime to a full menu for dinner, the restaurant is open every day and makes an ideal eating place whether staying at the hotel or just dining out. Cathrin and John are also offering a 10% discount off visitors' first night's accommodation when they book as a result of reading Hidden Places.

Just a couple of minutes walk from the centre of Porthmadog lies the popular public house and restaurant, **The Newborough Bach**. An attractive and distinctive black and white building, this pub is as pleasant and characterful inside as the exterior would suggest. Managed by Alison Jones since the summer of 1998, The Newborough Bach is open all day, every

**The Newborough Bach, New Street, Porthmadog
Gwynedd LL49 9ED Tel: 01766 512307**

day, and welcomes both locals and visitors to the town with warm and friendly hospitality. As well as the full selection of ales, beers, lagers, and ciders from the bar, the pub serves a tasty and extensive range of bar meals and snacks at both lunchtime and in the evening. Comfortable and cosy within, outside, and especially well used in the summer, there is an delightful beer garden for eating and drinking al fresco.

Just over half a mile from the town centre lies **Tyddyn Llwyn Caravan Park**, a delightful place situated in a saucer-shaped valley that is sheltered by woodland to the north and east. The valley is open to the south and

**Tyddyn Llwyn Caravan Park, Morfa Bychan, Porthmadog
Gwynedd LL49 9UR Tel: 01766 512205**

there are magnificent views across the rural countryside to Moel-y-Gest mountain. The site itself covers some 14 acres, but this is only part of the 50 acres of surrounding countryside and woodland through which those staying here can wander freely. Open from March to October and with hard and soft standing for around 150 touring caravans and tents, this well maintained and attractive park has been owned and personally run by Lon and Alun Roberts since 1995. As well as the usual facilities, the site has a launderette and a well stocked shop that provides all the camper could need for the perfect, relaxing holiday. Ideally located for exploring the Lleyn Peninsula, Snowdonia National Park, and the area's pretty villages, the site is the perfect place for a get-away-from-it-all break. Children are welcome and, as well as their own purpose built, safe play area, there is also a games room for them to enjoy. Dogs too are welcomed and the site has a dedicated dog walking area.

WEST OF PORTHMADOG

TREMADOG	MAP 2 REF E5
1 mile N of Porthmadog on A498	

This village, developed, like its close neighbour Porthmadog, by William Maddocks is a wonderful example of early 19th century town planning and contains many fine Regency buildings. The soldier and author TE Lawrence (of Arabia) was born here in 1888 and the poet Shelley is know to have visited Tremadog occasionally.

The Golden Fleece, a famous old coaching inn set in the heart of the village, is well known, far and wide, for the excellent food, ale, and hospitality it offers all its customers. Owned and personally run since the early 1970s by Jenny and Roger Jones, this charming late 19th century inn is as full of character and charm as its exterior promises and it also features a unique bar fashioned from the old brick cellar. Open every day, not only is this the place to come to for a full range of beers and ales but there is also a tasty range of bar snacks and meals on offer that can be eaten either in the bar, the cosy lounge, or in the lovely covered courtyard.

The Bistro restaurant is separate from the pub and, housed in the old stable block, is open every evening in the summer and at weekends in the winter. Here is served a delicious and varied menu that is sure to find favour with everyone. Those visiting the area will be pleased to learn that the inn also has four excellent guest rooms which provide all that is necessary for a peaceful and relaxing night's sleep. Finally, The Golden Fleece hosts an informal folk night every Tuesday evening and there is live jazz in the bistro on the first Thursday of the month. An ideal place to stay, eat, and drink whilst in the area, with both a friendly atmosphere and welcoming children.

The Golden Fleece, Tremadog, Gwynedd LL49 9RB
Tel: 01766 512421

PENMORFA   MAP 1 REF E5
2 miles W of Porthmadog on A487

In a range of old farm buildings, just southwest of Penmorfa, lies **Tyn Llan Crafts**, an interesting attraction that can be found in a quiet backwater at the end of a leafy lane. However, this road was once the main route to the Lleyn Peninsula and was frequented by both pilgrims and drovers. With a craft shop, full of wares from around the country, a small **Farm Museum**, and a café housed in the converted stables, which serves a range of home-made Welsh treats, this is a delightful place for all the family.

CRICCIETH   MAP 1 REF E5
4 miles W of Porthmadog on A497

This small family resort lies near the northeast corner of Cardigan Bay and enjoys fine views down the Lleyn coastline and northeast to Snowdonia. Unlike many of the other resorts on the peninsula, Criccieth has the look of a south coast seaside town.

The town's attractive Victorian demeanour is enhanced by **Criccieth Castle** which stands on a rocky outcrop, looming over the town and Tremadog Bay. A Welsh structure established between 1230 and 1240 by Llewelyn the Great, the castle's twin towered gatehouse is unique amongst Llewelyn's castles and may well have been copied from English buildings

Criccieth Castle

of the time. In 1283, the castle was taken by Edward I and extensively altered and enlarged - work which included the adaption of a tower for use by a catapult. However, having withstood a long siege, the castle was eventually taken by Owain Glyndwr in 1404 and its walls still bear the scorch marks caused by the fire that engulfed the building following its capture.

The wonderful **Poachers Restaurant**, in the heart of Criccieth, is hard to miss as it is painted green and there are a mass of flower filled tubs and window boxes decorating the exterior. Inside, the restaurant is a treat and it makes an attractive and characterful place to enjoy a delicious meal. Owned and personally run by Jill and Martin Bischoff, this charming couple have plenty of experience in the restaurant business: Martin's father was a chef and the couple met whilst Martin was working in Canada. A chef himself, Martin puts together a mouth-watering menu that combines the freshest of local produce with flavours from

**Poachers Restaurant, 66 High Street,
Criccieth, Gwynedd LL52 0HB
Tel: 01766 522512**

around the world. The house specialities are fish and vegetarian dishes and the freshly caught fish dishes are displayed on the ever changing blackboard. Open every evening throughout the summer and most evenings in the winter, this cosy and intimate restaurant is ideal for those who enjoy their food and appreciate the finer things in life at sensible prices.

Situated on the sea front, with panoramic views over Cardigan Bay to Harlech and Porthmadog in the east and Pwllheli in the west, **The Bay View Hotel** is very aptly named. Owned and personally run by Pauline and Pete Bennett, this attractive hotel was originally built as a private residence in the late 19th century and today, after a complete refurbishment, it provides visitors with comfortable accommodation. There are seven en-suite guest rooms, all furnished and decorated to a high standard, and many have magnificent sea views. Homely and relaxing, this friendly hotel not only offers guests a substantial breakfast that is certainly a feast but dinner, too, is a mouthwatering meal of delicious dishes. As the premises is also licensed, guests can relax in the cosy lounge and enjoy a quiet drink, before or after their meal, and reflect on the day's events. A charming and delightful place to stay, which sees many guests returning time and time again, The Bay View Hotel is an ideal choice for those visiting the Lleyn Peninsula. Guests should, however, remember that the hotel has a no smoking policy throughout.

The Bay View Hotel, 28 Marine Terrace, Criccieth, Gwynedd LL52 0EL Tel & Fax: 01766 522866

LLANYSTUMDWY

MAP 1 REF E5

6 miles W of Porthmadog off A497

This small coastal village is famous as being the home of David Lloyd George, the MP for Caernarfon for 55 years and a Prime Minister who not only had a reputation for reform at the beginning of the 20th century but

Llanystumdwy

also took the country through to the Armistice at the end of World War I. The **Lloyd George Museum** stands in the village in celebration of this great man and ,along with his tomb which was designed by Clough Williams-Ellis and can be found by the side of the River Dwyfor, makes an interesting and informative visit. **Highgate**, his boyhood cottage home, is also open to the public and, with its authentic Victorian interior, is just as it was when Lloyd George lived here.

LLANGYBI   MAP 1 REF E5
9 miles W of Porthmadog off A499

This village is home to **St Cybi's Well** and behind it the Iron Age fort, **Garn Pentyrch**. The well was established in the 6th century when St Cybi was in the process of setting up cells and a monastery in Holyhead. Sheltered by an unusual building with beehive vaulting that is thought to be unique in Wales, the well had a reputation for curing amongst other things blindness and warts.

BRYNCIR   MAP 1 REF E5
6 miles NW of Porthmadog on A487

To the east of the village can be found **Bryncir Woollen Mill**, set between the entrances to two wonderful valleys, Cwm Pennant and Cwm Ystradllyn.

Originally built as a corn mill in the mid 19th century, the mill was later converted to woollen manufacture and has been in continuous production ever since. A fascinating place to tour, after watching the spinning and weaving processes, visitors can purchase the finished articles, of which there are a great variety.

TREFOR   MAP 1 REF D5

13 miles W of Porthmadog off A499

This coastal village is dominated by **Yr Eifl** (The Forks), which lies to the southwest and from the 1850 foot summit of which are stunning views out over to Anglesey and across the Lleyn peninsula. On the eastern side, lies **Tre'r Ceiri** (Town of Giants), one of the finest Iron Age forts in Britain. A stone wall surrounds this seemingly once heavily populated circle of roughly 150 huts.

The road between Trefor and Clynnog Fawr, to the northeast, passes by the ancient looking **Bwlch Mawr** and **Gurn Ddu** hills, that sweep down towards the sandy beach.

From its elevated position, **Plas yr Eifl Hotel** has a wonderful outlook over the sea and the mountains of the Lleyn Peninsula provide a backdrop in the opposite direction. Built at the turn of the century as a substantial private house, Plas yr Eifl is now a charming, family hotel owned and personally run by Linda and George Newsham with the help of Linda's mother Betty. As well as the 10 comfortable en-suite guest bedrooms, the hotel has a fine restaurant and cosy bar that are both open to non-residents. Full of memorabilia relating to the village and surrounding area, the bar is open at lunchtime and in the evening during the summer and serves a fine range of ales and beers.

**Plas yr Eifl Hotel, Trefor, Caernarfon, Gwynedd LL54 5NA
Tel: 01286 660781**

The attractive restaurant, with views over the sea, has an enviable reputation in the area for the high standard of its cuisine and, in particular, its seafood and fish dishes. Freshly prepared to order, the hotel's chef takes pride in offering an unusually cosmopolitan menu that is complemented by a comprehensive wine list. Finally, Plas yr Eifl Hotel is also popular with divers, who can choose to either use the sea or a local large man-made lake formed after a quarry was flooded. Those coming here for a diving holiday, whether beginners or experienced divers, may be interested to learn that the hotel also has two bunkhouses on the premises.

CLYNNOG FAWR   MAP 1 REF D4
11 miles NW of Porthmadog on A499

This typical Lleyn village is famous for **St Beuno's Church** that stands on the original site of a chapel that was founded by the saint in about AD 616. St Beuno's burial place and his shrine can be seen in this early 16th-century church which lies on the Pilgrims' Route to Bardsey Island. St Beuno's tomb was thought, for many years, to have curative powers.

The nearby **St Beuno's Well** was also thought to help cure illnesses, especially if the sufferer had first visited the church. Close by, virtually on the seafront, stands the capstone and three uprights of **Bachwen**, a Neolithic burial chamber.

Standing in its own private one and a half acres of garden, **Bryn Eisteddfod Hotel and Restaurant** is a charming family run establishment that has been owned by Jan and David Allen since 1996. This large and grand Victorian house was built in the late 19th century for a local minis-

**Bryn Eisteddfod Hotel and Restaurant, Clynnog Fawr, Caernarfon
Gwynedd LL54 5DA Tel & Fax: 01286 660431**

ter with 10 children and, as well as being spacious there are panoramic views over the Rivals Mountains to the south and the Isle of Anglesey to the north. Excellent accommodation is provided in a choice of eight guest rooms that provide a level of comfort and luxury that makes for a truly peaceful and relaxing holiday.

The hotel's restaurant, open to non-residents from Tuesday to Saturday evenings, is found in a charming conservatory to the rear of the hotel that overlooks the beautiful landscaped grounds. Fresh local produce and home-cooking are very much the watchwords of the restaurant and the à la carte menu is an imaginative list of delicious dishes that make the best of Welsh meat, game, fish, and vegetables. Add to this the tasty bar menu, the blackboard list of daily specials, the varied wine list and it is not surprising that the restaurant has an enviable reputation and is very popular. Guests to the hotel and those just visiting the restaurant also receive a welcome that is both warm and friendly and which puts the finishing touch to this delightful establishment.

Bordered on one side by the sea and with a backdrop provided by the Rivals Mountain range, **Parsal Caravan and Camping Park** has a truly magnificent position. Part of the small working farm, the site, which occupies some seven acres, is owned and personally run by Arthur and Josie. Open from March to the end of the October, this superb park not only has three six-berth static caravans for hire but there is also plenty of room for 27 touring caravans and 20 tents. As well as the usual facilities, there is a safe play area and direct access onto a safe beach for swimming, with sand and rock pool at low water. Children and small pets are welcome and this wonderful site offers not only a relaxing and tranquil holiday base but also the opportunity to witness some amazing sun sets over the sea.

Parsal Caravan and Camping Park, Parsal, Clynnog Fawr
Gwynedd LL54 5PS Tel: 01286 660222

TAI-IÔN
MAP 1 REF E4

10 miles NW of Porthmadog off A487

Here the **Museum of Welsh Country Life** enjoys an attractive setting by the River Desach. Featuring a variety of bygone themes, the museum is housed in a 17th century water-mill.

PENYGROES
MAP 1 REF E4

11 miles NW of Porthmadog on A487

The last surviving fully operational slate works in North Wales, **Inigo Jones Slateworks**, just northwest of Penygroes, is a fascinating place to visit. First opened in 1861, the works have been supplying slate products to the four corners of the world ever since and, today, visitors can tour the workshops and watch the skill of the craftsmen as they fashion the slate. The historical exhibition gives an insight into the development of the industry whilst, in the lettercutting workshop, there is the opportunity for visitors to try their hand at engraving for themselves. With plenty of interest for children and a superb craft showroom, these slate works make an enjoyable and unusual day out for all the family.

LLANDWROG
MAP 1 REF E4

13 miles NW of Porthmadog off A499

Originally, an estate village built by Lord Newborough for Glynllifon Park, the village is associated with an interesting but gruesome tale. One night, a midwife of Llandwrog was called out by a mysterious stranger, who carried her on horseback to a wonderful underground castle, to assist a beautiful queen in childbirth. The stranger gave the midwife some ointment to anoint the baby's eyes but warned her not to touch her own eyes with the cream. She did so accidentally and the scene suddenly changed: the castle became a cave and the queen became her former serving maid. Some weeks later, the midwife saw the stranger at Caernarfon market and asked after the health of her serving maid. After replying that all was well, the stranger asked the midwife which eye she saw him with. When she answered, he took a rush and poked the eye out!

DINAS DINLLE
MAP 1 REF E4

14 miles W of Porthmadog off A499

With a shingle beach and cliffs, there are many pleasant spots to picnic and enjoy the view down the north coast of the peninsula from the village. At the beach's northerly tip lies **Fort Belan**, built in the 18th century along with nearby **Fort Williamsburg**, was built by the first Lord Newborough, who felt concerned enough about the threat of Napoleon and the French. The Royal Caernarfonshire Grenadiers, the Lord's private army, was a force of 400 men raised and equipped at his own expense which had, by the time of his death in 1807, cost the Lord a quarter of his fortune.

Also at Dinas Dinlle is **Caernarfon Air World** which tells something of the history of aviation as well as offering hands-on experience of a plane's cockpit. The RAF used the base during World War II and, though the field is now used by private craft, a great lure for the visitor is the chance to enjoy a pleasure flight in a vintage De Havilland Rapide. Open daily from March to November this is a tremendous opportunity to see North Wales from an unusual viewpoint.

SOUTH OF PORTHMADOG

BORTH-Y-GEST   MAP 2 REF E5
1 mile S of Porthmadog on A487

A pleasant and quiet village by the sea that is in sharp contrast to the hustle and bustle of Porthmadog. Boats and yachts lie in the small bay and seafront cafés offer the chance to soak up the atmosphere in a more leisurely fashion. Walks along the sea or up **Moel-y-Gest**, which was once the site of a fort, offer wonderful panoramic views of the area and across Tremadog Bay.

PORTMEIRION   MAP 2 REF F5
2 miles S of Porthmadog on A487

Now a National Trust property, the village, in a wonderful setting, was once owned by Sir Clough Williams-Ellis who conceived and created this magical place between 1925 and 1972 on the quiet peninsula where the estuaries of the Rivers Glaslyn and Dwyryd meet. Fifty or so buildings, some consisting only of the frontal façade, were inspired by a visit of Williams-Ellis to Sorrento in Italy. In the central Piazza, theatre productions are put on during the summer months and the firework displays when on are quite spectacular.

The village also has shops selling the famous **Portmeirion Pottery** amongst other things and the Terrace Restaurant serves a variety of snacks and lunches. The Hotel burnt down in 1981 has been restored to its former glory and is open to non-residents. The television series *The Prisoner* was made in the village and wandering around the delightful woodland and secluded beaches those familiar with the programme will recognise the locations.

It is worth remembering that the tidal currents from the estuaries make bathing here precarious and therefore great care must be taken. However, do not be discouraged from making the effort as the village is a pleasant

Portmeirion

day out with ideal picnic spots dotted around the beaches and woodland.

Williams-Ellis' ancestral home, **Plas Brondanw**, lies some five miles away, up the A4085, where the marvellous gardens alone make it worth a visit.

PENRHYNDEUDRAETH   MAP 2 REF F5
3 miles E of Porthmadog on A487

Lying at the foot of the Vale of Ffestiniog, Penrhyndeudraeth is a small, unassuming town. The tollbridge over the River Dwyryd connects the town with the south, whilst it can be reached from Porthmadog by another tollbridge over the sands. During a crossing at low tide herons, curlews, and terns can be seen feeding on the sandbanks.

ABERSOCH

This is a popular, family resort with safe beaches found on each side of the estuary of the River Soch located towards the tip of the Lleyn peninsula. It's harbour attracts pleasure craft and out to sea lie **St Tudwal's Islands** called so because Tugdual founded a religious cell here in the 6th century; both islands are now privately owned and the home of bird sanctuaries.

The site of the 17th-century mansion, **Castellmarch**, was said to be the home of March Amheirchion, one of King Arthur's Knights. Reputedly to have the ears of a horse, March (the name is Welsh for horse) kept them hidden and killed anyone who saw them, burying the bodies in a nearby reed bed. A young man, cutting reeds to make himself a flute, discovered the deformity when he found that the only song the flute could play was *March Amheirchion has horse's ears*!

NORTH AND WEST OF ABERSOCH

LLANBEDROG
MAP 1 REF D6

3 miles N of Abersoch on A499

Named after the 6th century St Pedrog, Llanbedrog lies on the other side of **Myndd Tir y Cwmwd** from Abersoch and from which there is a footpath to the top guaranteeing glorious views over the peninsula and out to sea. On the summit is the **Tin Man**, a modern sculpture made of beachcombed material which faces towards Snowdonia.

In Llanbedrog itself, **Plas Glyn-y-Weddw**, a Gothic mansion that has a fine collection of Welsh furniture and art on display, makes an interesting and informative visit.

PWLLHELI
MAP 1 REF D5

6 miles N of Abersoch on A499

Pronounced Pool-thelli, the name translates to Salt Water Pool. Like Nefyn, its near neighbour on the north coast of peninsula, Pwllheli was granted a charter in 1355 and Pwllheli has, traditionally, been the area's the main town as well as being another popular holiday resort. Markets are still held here on Wednesdays, where local produce amongst other things are worth seeking out, but the harbour, which once handled sea going traffic, is now used by small pleasure craft.

On the road inland is **Bodvell Hall Adventure Park**, a family orientated centre with birds of prey, adventure playgrounds, a farmyard, and nature trails. Bodvell Hall itself was the birthplace of Mrs Thrale, a close friend of the diarist, Dr Johnson. Also close by is **Butlins Holiday World - Starcoast World**, where day visits are encouraged; a useful place for those with children should the weather turn foul. In complete contrast, almost opposite and perhaps a mile up a country road from the holiday camp, is **Penarth Fawr**, a 15th-century manor house owned by Cadw Welsh Historic Monuments.

The Black Lion, in the heart of this popular town, dates back to the mid 18th century when it was a coaching inn with its own smithy. Today, this well frequented inn is personally run by Jane and Wilf Childes, with the help of their son Jason, and before coming here in the summer of 1998, the couple were stewards at Pwllheli Golf Club. A traditional public house serving a range of beers, ales, lagers, and wines, the interior is olde

**The Black Lion, Abererch Road, Pwllheli, Gwynedd LL53 5LE
Tel: 01758 612315**

worlde in appearance and, in the lounge bar, there are numerous prints, photographs, and other memorabilia about the area's two famous RAF bases, Penrhos and Hellsmouth. Open all day, every day, this is a relaxing and friendly place for a quiet pint of beer. However, this is not all this charming pub has to offer as, in the true tradition of an inn, there is a splendid menu of tasty bar snacks and meals from which to choose that can be eaten either in the bar or in the separate restaurant area. Finally, for those who enjoy testing their general knowledge, there is a fun quiz, open to everyone, each Thursday evening.

NEFYN   MAP 1 REF D5
8 miles N of Abersoch on B4417

This resort, once a fishing village, was granted a charter in 1355, along with Pwllheli, by the Black Prince. Earlier, in 1284, Edward I celebrated his conquest over Wales here.

TUDWEILIOG   MAP 1 REF C5
7 miles N of Abersoch on B4417

The village is centrally placed on a rugged length of coastline that is broken by a variety of small bays, Porths Towyn, Ysglaig, Ysgaden, and Gwylan. Though access is difficult they are well worth visiting.

BOTWNNOG
MAP 1 REF C6
4 miles W of Abersoch on B4413

This village's church is dedicated to St Beuno and it contains timber from an Italian shipwreck. Close to the village are the remains of a heavily populated hill fort on **Carn Fadryn**. The fort is known as the 'castle of the sons of Owain'.

METHLEM
MAP 1 REF C6
8 miles W of Abersoch off B4413

The curiously named **Porth-oer** (Whistling Sands) are worth a visit as the sands literally whistle when walked upon. Apparently the noise is caused by the rubbing together of minute quartz granules.

ABERDARON
MAP 1 REF C6
8 miles W of Abersoch on B4413

This small, delightful village is often busy at the height of summer and has a variety of places to stay and eat. The Tripartite Indenture was signed in Aberdaron in 1405 - it was an agreement to divide Britain with Wales becoming independent under the rule of Glyndwr whilst the Percies and Mortimers would split the north and south. These plans were ruined by Henry IV and Henry V.

St Hywyn's Church, which stands close to the sea and originally dates from the 6th century, was thought to have sheltered the 12th-century Prince of Wales, Gryffydd ap Rhys from marauding Saxons, as well as Cromwell's men later on during the Civil War.

However, perhaps Aberdaron's most famous native is Richard Roberts Jones, the son of a local carpenter. He was a strange vagabond, known as Dic Aberdaron, and a natural self-educated linguist who is said to have spoken 35 languages and is renowned for having compiled a dictionary in Welsh, Greek, and Hebrew.

Roughly a mile or so out of the village lies **Castell Odo**, an Iron Age fort and the first to be excavated in the peninsula. Its discovery and subsequent study led archaeologists to realise that perhaps there were five different occupations of the area from as far back as the 4th century BC. There is also some speculation as to whether this was the first Celtic settlement in North Wales.

The surrounding countryside is quite delightful and full of more surprises; **Bodwrdda**, a private Tudor house lies by the River Daron and, out to sea, are the islands of *Ynys Gwylan-fawr* which serve as sanctuaries for birdlife. **Porth Ysgo** is attractive National Trust land with a calming waterfall dropping down towards the sea.

Y Gegin Fawr, Aberdaron, Pwllheli, Gwynedd LL53 8BE
Tel: 01758 760359

Perhaps the most interesting building in the village is **Y Gegin Fawr**, a one time medieval resting place for pilgrims on their way to Bardsey Island that is now a café. Owned and personally run by Karen and Colin Wisbey, this attractive and obviously old building has been beautifully furnished and decorated to offer customers a comfortable and welcome surroundings in which to try the café's delicious fare. Open seven days a week from Easter to the end of October, the menu at Y Gegin Fawr caters for all tastes. There are a mouth-watering array of home-made cakes and the light lunches and afternoon teas include a whole range of freshly prepared dishes: the house speciality is fish and, in particular, locally caught crab and lobster. All the family are welcome at Y Gegin Fawr and there is outdoor seating for those warm summer days.

BRAICH-Y-PWLL   MAP 1 REF C6
10 miles W of Abersoch off B4413

This headland, owned by the National Trust, gives terrific views over Bardsey Sound to Bardsey Island, the holy island. A footpath leads down Braich-y-Pwll to **Ffynnon Ffair (St Mary's Well)** below. The well is covered at high tide but the water remains strangely pure.

BARDSEY ISLAND   MAP 1 REF B6
12 miles W of Abersoch

Settlement of the island is thought to have begun during the Dark Ages. It was the death of St Dyfrig on the island that saw the beginning of the pilgrimages and it was thought that three pilgrimages to Bardsey were equal to one to Rome. Little remains of the monastery that was begun in the 12th century and the island is now an important bird and field observatory. Boat trips around the island can be made from Aberdaron.

The island's name is Norse in origin and the Welsh name, **Ynys Enlii**, means Island of Currents - reference to the turbulent waters between the holy island and the mainland. Mainlanders were known to report shadowy figures wandering along its shores; the 'ghosts' were said to be omens of disease, drowning, and storms.

RHIW   MAP 1 REF C6
5 miles W of Abersoch off B4413

This hamlet lies on a miniature pass and overlooks **Porth Neigwl** (Hell's Mouth) a four mile sweep of beach so called because of its reputation for strong currents.

Protected from the Atlantic gales by Mynydd Rhiw, **Plas yn Rhiw** is a small, part medieval, part Tudor, and part Georgian manor house. Given to the National Trust by the Keating sisters in 1952, it stands in some 60 acres of woodland and gardens and faces the sea. The Keating sisters, Lorna and Honora, bought the property in 1938 and lovingly restored it after the house had been neglected for some 20 years. Tirelessly working to protect the natural beauty of the peninsula, they were often seen tramping down the lanes to check rubbish tips and illegal caravan sites.

LLANENGAN   MAP 1 REF D6
1 mile W of Abersoch off A499

The village church contains relics reputed to have come from the abbey on Bardsey Island after the Dissolution.

4 Isle of Anglesey

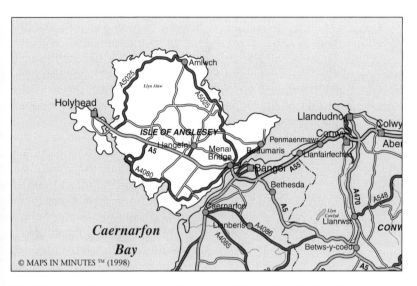

© MAPS IN MINUTES ™ (1998)

The Isle of Anglesey, with its rolling, low hills and fertile farmland, comes as something of a surprise after the dramatic, rugged landscape of North Wales. Its craggy and at times wild coastline, dotted with sandy coves and bays, can be as seductive as any other place in Britain for the interested visitor.

This island, of roughly 275 square miles, has attracted settlers from the Stone Age onwards and the evidence of their, and subsequent, occupations is all around. The first visitors to the island were Neolithic people and their presence is felt to this day in the remains of many burial chambers dotted around the island: Barclodiad y Gawres, for instance, on the southwestern coast, is a fine example of stonework from those times. Later, during the Bronze Age, mineral wealth was found in Parys Mountain and used to make weapons whilst also increasing the power of the inhabitants. Close to Gaerwen, burial urns from those times have been found.

The Romans came to Anglesey and were forced to attack twice before defeating the Iron Age chiefs in AD 79. After their withdrawal, the local language and culture returned and only the remains of Roman fortress sites bear witness to their time on the island. From the 7th to the 13th century, the kings of Gwynedd ruled from Aberffraw but, unfortunately, there is little evidence of their reigns today. Like other areas of Wales,

Anglesey felt the force and influence of Edward I's invasion of the country; his physical presence is still to be seen in the impressive Beaumaris Castle.

Anglesey is known as the 'Mother of Wales' (the name in Welsh is Ynys Môn), so called because of the island's mild, favourable climate. Farmers grew grain crops which were sent to sustain the settlements in the bleak Welsh interior.

A popular holiday destination, with many charming Victorian seaside resorts, Anglesey is also a popular place for bird enthusiasts. With the opportunity to see sea-birds in their natural habitat the island is also alive with animal and plant life. As well as offering sights of natural and historical interest, the nuclear age has also reached the island. Wylfa Power Station, just to the north of the hamlet of Tregele, has an information centre with guided tours and is open to the public daily.

MENAI BRIDGE

This largely Victorian town developed after the construction of **Telford's Bridge** which connects the island to the mainland. Acting as a gateway to Anglesey, the waterfront is a popular place for anglers and for those wishing to view the Regatta on the Strait which takes place on these sheltered waters every August.

Telford's Menai Suspension Bridge

On **Church Island**, reached by a causeway from the town, there is a small 14th-century church built on the site of a foundation by St Tysilio in AD 630. The site is thought to have been visited by Archbishop Baldwin and Giraldus when they may have landed here in 1188.

For a place with a difference, **Pili Palas (Butterfly Palace)** is an interesting and unusual attraction that will delight everyone. The vast collection of butterflies from all over the world are housed in a tropical environment, where visitors can not only enjoy the colourful creatures flying around but also the exotic plants and other tropical beasts found here.

NORTH OF MENAI BRIDGE

BEAUMARIS   Map 2 ref F3
5 miles NE of Menai Bridge on A545

This attractive and elegant town contains many interesting places to see and visit. Granted a charter by Edward in 1294 the town adopted the Norman name 'beau marais' which translates as beautiful marsh. The lawned seafront with its elegant Georgian and Victorian terraces was once a marsh that protected the approaches to **Beaumaris Castle**. The last of Edward I's eight castles, this is perhaps the most becoming of them all. Virtually surrounded by its original moat, there was also a tidal dock for ships coming in through a channel in the marshes - an iron ring where vessels of up to 40 tons once docked still hangs from the wall. The castle is regarded as a pinnacle of military architecture of the time and it is designed with a concentric defence rather than the traditional keep and bailey. The outer walls contain 16 towers whilst the inner walls were 43 feet high and 16 feet thick in places. Perhaps a measure of the castle's success was that, unlike other castles built by Edward, it never experienced military action and was, in fact, never completed in its entirety.

Having said that, Beaumaris did, for a period of time, enjoy a notoriety as being a haven for pirates as well as a busy trading port. With the advent of steam ships and paddle boats, the resort's elegance developed during Victorian times as visitors from Liverpool and elsewhere took the sea trip down to Beaumaris. The town is now a popular place for the yachting fraternity with its facilities and involvement in the **Menai Strait Regatta**.

The **Beaumaris Court and Gaol** is an interesting place to step back in time as well as reflect on how fortunate we are to live in more civilised times today. The Courthouse was built in 1614 and, despite being renovated in the 19th century, much of its original structure still remains. Visitors can stand in the dock where, in 1773, Mary Hughes was sentenced to be transported for seven years after being found guilty of stealing a bed gown valued at six pence! Within the gaol, the punishment and condemned cells can be viewed as well as following the route a condemned man would have taken to the scaffold. Opened in 1973 and with something to delight and fascinate all ages, the **Museum of Childhood Memories** represents another step back in time for all who visit. Housed in two adjoining buildings and with themed rooms, the amazing variety of toys and amusements are not only interesting but they also illustrate the changing habits of the nation over the last 150 years.

**Henllys Hall Hotel, Beaumaris, Anglesey LL58 8HU
Tel: 01248 810412 Fax: 01248 811511**

Henllys Hall Hotel, undoubtedly one of the top hotels on Anglesey, is certainly the place for visitors with sumptuous tastes and for those looking for the ideal country retreat. Set in 125 acres of woodland overlooking the Menai Straits, this magnificent establishment can trace its history back to the days of Llewelyn the Great in the 13th century. There are 23 beautifully furnished en-suite bedrooms, many with a four-poster bed to add a touch of romance, and all with fine views over the estate and the surrounding countryside. On chillier days, guests can relax in front of a log fire in the cosy lounge before making their way into the intimate elegance of the restaurant where there is a fine choice of menu with a wine list to match. As well as the hotel's excellent health and fitness centre and outdoor heated swimming pool, Henllys Hall Hotel also has a challenging 18-hole golf course, The Princes' Golf Course. Open to non-residents, the course makes full use of the mature parkland and natural water hazards of the estate and, with the Menai Straits and Snowdonia Mountains providing a backdrop, this must be one of the more picturesque courses in the area.

LLANFAES
5 miles N of Menai Bridge on B5109

MAP 2 REF E3

Despite its sedate demeanour Llanfaes was once a busy commercial village before the establishment of Beaumaris and travellers from the mainland arrived here after crossing from Aber and the Lavan Sands. In 1237 Llewelyn the Great founded a monastery in the village over the tomb of Joan, his wife and daughter of King John. The tomb is now to be found in St Mary's

Church in Beaumaris. During Edward I's reign the inhabitants of Llanfaes were forcibly removed to settle in Newborough on the east side of the island. During World War Two, flying boats were built at the factory by the village.

LLANGOED
MAP 2 REF F3

7 miles N of Menai Bridge on B5109

This historic village was, in Edwardian times, a popular resort with the lower middle classes who came here to relax in a boarding house by the sea.

Llangoed's charm is enhanced by its pastoral setting where a walk downstream, alongside the river, leads to **Castell Aber Lleiniog**, found in a midst of trees. This was, originally, a timber castle built in around 1090 by Hugh Lupus, Earl of Chester who, along with Hugh the Proud, Earl of Shrewsbury exacted great cruelty on the Welsh. He was later killed during an attack on the castle by Magnus, King of Norway, when he was struck in the eye by an arrow. The ruins of a bailey, which was constructed later, are still visible. Close by is the site of a battle where in 809, the Saxons were, briefly, victorious over the defending Welsh.

PENMON
MAP 2 REF F2

8 miles N of Menai Bridge off B5109

This is a beauty spot whose lovely views across the Strait go some way to explaining why it was chosen, centuries earlier, as a religious site. **Penmon Priory** and **St Seiriol's Church**, part of a religious settlement that dates back to the 6th century, can still be seen here. The church, which was rebuilt in the 12th century, has wonderful examples of Norman architecture and a carved cross, recently moved to the church from the fields nearby, shows influences from Scandinavia and Ireland. A dovecote built around 1600 by Sir Richard Bulkeley contains nearly 1000 pigeon holes. Other buildings around the church date from the 6th century onwards. Nearby a path runs by the monastery's old fish pond before arriving at the foundations of **St Seiriol's Well** where converts where baptised.

The abandoned quarry, close to the village, once provided stone for Beaumaris Castle as well as the Telford and Stephenson bridges.

PUFFIN ISLAND
MAP 2 REF F2

9 miles N of Menai Bridge

The home of the remains of St Seiriol's sanctuary, Puffin Island is thought once to have been connected to the mainland. St Seiriol was said to have a chapel across the bay in Penmaenmawr and records tell of journeys between the two. The isle, known in Welsh as Ynys Seiriol, was so called because of the puffins who nested here. The numbers did decline during the 19th century due to rats and also because the young birds were considered a delicacy when pickled.

PENTRAETH   MAP 1 REF E3
4 miles N of Menai Bridge on A5025

This sleepy village was, before land reclamation, on the edge of Red Wharf Bay. At low tide there are virtually 15 square miles of sand in this bay on which a cockles industry once flourished. Nowadays, this is a popular spot for holiday-makers although it is not ideal for swimming due to strong tidal currents.

Close to **Plas Gwyn**, a 18th-century Georgian mansion, is the **Three Leaps** - three stones that commemorate a traditional contest between two lovers for the hand of a girl. The contest was won by the one who could leap furthest, in this case, an individual named Howel. The stones mark his efforts whilst the loser was said to have died of a broken heart.

Stone Science, to the west of the village, is a most unusual attraction that takes visitors back in time, to 650 million years ago, and the world of fossils, rocks, and dinosaurs.

Dating back to the mid 18th century, **The Bull Inn**, in the heart of Pentraeth, was at one time a coaching and posting inn. Until recently the pub had taken a turn for the worst and was in a slow decline but, thanks to Peter Jones, who arrived here in August 1998, things have certainly begun to pick up. As Peter has started to put his plans for the pub into operation, The Bull Inn is once again becoming a popular place locally and with visitors. There is an ever changing selection of real ales from the bar and also an excellent wine list taken from around the world. Open every day,

The Bull Inn, Pentraeth, Anglesey LL75 8LJ
Tel: 01248 450232

and all day at the weekends, there is live music on Friday and Saturday evenings and pub quizzes during the winter.

However, the biggest change that Peter has made here has been in the restaurant. His appointment of Guillermo Camara, a well respected local chef, and Marcus Walsh as an assistant, ensures that the meals served here will be of the highest quality and this team is sure to put The Bull Inn on the culinary map of Wales. Using only local, fresh food, from Welsh black beef and locally caught fish to Welsh butter, milk, and even mineral water, the imaginative and varied menu of international dishes all have a genuine Welsh slant. Cooked to order and beautifully presented, a meal in the restaurant here is one to savour.

Found at **Llanbedrgoch**, just north of Pentraeth, and in the heart of open countryside, not far from the east coast beaches, **Ty Newydd Leisure Park** is an excellent caravan park that offers holidaymakers the perfect opportunity for a peaceful and relaxing stay. Owned and personally run by Gill and Mike Monger since the late 1970s, this family orientated park covers some nine acres of parkland and has been laid out to ensure that everyone has plenty of space and privacy. As well as taking touring caravans and campers with a choice of hard and soft standing and electricity supply, there are also a number of privately owned static caravans here, some of which are available for hire.

Ty Newydd Leisure Park, Llanbedrgoch, Anglesey LL76 8TZ
Tel: 01248 450677 Fax: 01248 450711

An ideal place for all the family, Ty Newydd has a superb range of facilities which includes a well stocked site shop. There is a large heated outdoor swimming pool, with a surrounding patio area complete with sunloungers and chairs, and children can amuse themselves in the games room or in the safe purpose built playground. The fitness centre offers holidaymakers the chance to keep in shape and work off some of the excesses whilst, also at the country club, there is an excellent bar that serves a range of tasty snacks in the evening. Finally, the restaurant, which is open to non-residents, ensures that even the family cook can have a holiday away from the kitchen. The caravan park is open throughout the season whilst the country club is open throughout the year.

BENLLECH   MAP 1 REF E2
7 miles NW of Menai Bridge on A5025

This is probably the most popular resort on the island as holidaymakers are attracted to the town because of its good beach, though care should be as there are strong tidal currents and the sands can be treacherous. The resort was also the birthplace of the poet Goronwy Owen.

Traces of a hill fort, **Castell Mawr**, can be found on the west side of Red Wharf Bay, near Benllech, and on the evidence of coins found here, the site could once have been occupied by the Romans.

Found in the heart of Benllech, **The Glanarafon Hotel** is a distinctive mid 18th-century building that is hard to miss. It is also the place to come to for excellent food, drink, accommodation, and hospitality all of which is provided by the hosts, Chris and Heather. Well decorated and furnished, this delightful hotel offers customers a choice of 18 en-suite rooms, some of which have a sea view, in pleasant and comfortable surroundings. There

**The Glanarafon Hotel, Bangor Road, Benllech, Anglesey LL74 8TF
Tel: 01248 852364**

are two well stocked bars, open to non-residents, and as well as serving a full range of drinks, there are also Lee's traditional ales available. Dining here too is a pleasure and a full range of meals, from light snacks to full à la carte are served either in the bar or in the more formal dining room. It is advisable to book, particularly for the popular Sunday carvery. Entertainment also plays an important part in the life of the hotel and there is something most evenings, from a quiz on Tuesdays to live music at the weekend as well as Welsh singing and the separate disco in the River Room.

Found overlooking both Benllech Bay and the sandy beach of Treath Bychan, the **Beauchelles Hotel** is a delightful family orientated establishment that is owned and personally run by Lesley and Ronald Boshell. Dating back to the turn of the century and originally built for a wealthy ship's captain, this striking and attractive hotel offers guests comfortable accommodation in a choice of 12 en-suite rooms. The high standards of hospitality certainly do not end with the well furnished and decorated

Beauchelles Hotel, Benllech Bay, Anglesey LL73 8PL
Tel: 01248 853235 Fax: 01248 852086

guest rooms. Open all day, every day, the restaurant caters for all tastes from set three course lunches through to full à la carte and children's menus. For less formal eating there is the popular café bar which, too, is open all day. Entertainment, for all the family, also comes high on the list at the Beauchelles Hotel and children again are well catered for with a superb adventure playground and their own evening entertainment. A popular place locally as the restaurant and bar are open to non-residents, this hotel is not just a place to come to for good food and its selection of real ales and beers, but also for the live music and dancing that features most evenings.

MOELFRE   MAP 1 REF E2
9 miles NW of Menai Bridge on A5025

This is a charming coastal village with a sheltered, pebbled beach, attractive cottages, and sandy beaches to the north and south. Fame, however, came to Moelfre in an unfortunate and bizarre way via its lifeboat which, in its time, had been involved in many rescues, but there are two that particularly stand out. *The Royal Charter* returning to Liverpool from Australia in October 1859, laden with cargo and passengers, that included gold prospectors coming home after making their fortunes in the Australian Gold Rush, sank. The ship, a rigged iron vessel and the pride of the merchant fleet of the time, was to make the passage in record time. Four hundred and thirty people were drowned as the ship, sheltering in Moelfre Bay from a hurricane, floundered. Only 39 survived and many believe that the gold still lies within the wreck.

Efforts have been made to recover the fortune with varying but not overwhelming success. It has been said that the larger houses around Moelfre where paid for by gold washed ashore from the wreck; despite the fact that Customs Officers swamped the village in attempts to ensure that the gold ended in the Exchequer rather than the hands of locals. Charles Dickens visited the site on December 31st 1859 and apparently based a story on the disaster in the *Uncommercial Traveller*.

One hundred years later, in October 1959, the coaster *HINDLEA*, struggling in foul weather, had eight crew members rescued by the Moelfre Lifeboat. The rescue earned Richard Evans, the lifeboat's coxswain, the RNLI gold medal for gallantry for the second time.

Beyond the station is a small outcrop of rocks, **Ynys Moelfre**, a favourite spot for seabirds and the fortunate may be lucky enough to see a porpoise lingering in the bay. Perhaps a mile back off a narrow road leading out of the village is the impressive **Lligwy Burial Chamber**. A Bronze Age tomb that has a huge capstone supported by stone uprights, the tomb lies half hidden in a pit dug out of the rock. Close by is **Din Lligwy Village**, the remains of an ancient settlement, and some of the stone walls can still be seen standing to around six foot high and dating from the early Roman period. Pottery, coins and evidence of metal working from that period have been uncovered in this area. Also nearby are the ruins of the 14th-century **Capel Lligwy**.

LLANGEFNI   MAP 1 REF E3
5 miles W of Menai Bridge on B5420

The island's administrative centre, Llangefni is a busy market town with cattle markets on Wednesdays and a general one on both Thursdays and Saturdays. The cattle market is interesting if only to glimpse at a slice of rural life as the farmers meet, talk, and barter, comparing and considering the livestock on sale. **Oriel Ynys Môn** is an attractive art gallery and heritage centre which also tells the story of Anglesey, from prehistoric times to the present day, through a series of themes including Stone Age Hunters, Druids, Medieval Society, and Legends.

Cefni Reservoir to the northwest of the town is an important wildfowl habitat and also provides a pleasant picnic area.

WEST OF MENAI BRIDGE

LLANFAIR PG   MAP 1 REF E3
1 mile W of Menai Bridge on A4080

Llanfairpwllgwyngyll, often called Llanfair PG, is better known as the village with the world's longest placename. The full, tongue-twisting name is: Llanfairpwllgwyngyllgogerychwyrndrobwyll-llantysiliogogogh and translated it apparently means 'St Mary's Church in a hollow of white hazel near to a rapid whirlpool and St Tysilio's Church near the red cave'. The name is said to have been invented, in humorous reference to the burgeoning tourist trade, by a local man. It, however, did the trick, as many visitors stopped by initially, perhaps out of curiosity, but then maybe pleased by what they found here.

The village, lying by the Menai Strait, is where the Britannia Bridge crosses to the mainland (at the railway station the longest platform ticket in Britain can be purchased) and the **Marquis of Anglesey Column** looks out towards Snowdonia. The quiet splendid views from the top of the column are available to anyone wishing to pay a small fee and negotiating a spiral staircase consisting some 115 steps. Finished two years after the battle of Waterloo in 1815, the statue on top of the column was added in 1860 after the death of Henry Paget, the first Marquis of Anglesey whom it commemorates. Paget fought alongside Wellington at Waterloo where he lost a leg to one of the last shots fired in the battle.

The last public toll house stands in the village displaying the original tolls charged in 1895, the year it closed. Next door is the modest building where the Women's Institute was founded in 1915.

The **Carreg Bran Hotel** can be found on the outskirts of Llanfairpwllgwyngyll and close to the famous Britannia Bridge. This impressive first class hotel has been owned by Mrs N Edwards for the past 23 years and it is personally run by Mr Llewelyn, the manager, and his team of friendly and efficient staff. Attractively decorated and comfortably furnished throughout, the hotel boasts 29 en-suite guest rooms, a cosy bar area, delightful gardens, and a large function room that proves popular with wedding parties. The same high standards of service and comfort are

**The Carreg Bran Hotel, Church Lane, Llanfairpwllgwyngyll
Anglesey LL61 5YH Tel: 01248 714224 Fax: 01248 715983**

extended into the hotel's restaurant, where, in pleasant surroundings, guests and non-residents can enjoy a gourmet meal from either the table d'hôte or the à la carte menu. A popular and well regarded local restaurant, that is open every day for both lunch and dinner, it is advisable to book at weekends to avoid disappointment.

RHOSCOLYN   MAP 1 REF C3
17 miles W of Menai Bridge off A5

Enjoying a wide sandy beach which is good for swimming and fishing, this village was once home to a thriving oyster industry that is now sadly in decline. China clay was once quarried here and local marble was used in the building of Worcester, Bristol, and Peterborough cathedrals.

St Gwenfaen founded a church here in the 6th century and her well, on **Rhoscolyn Head**, was said to have properties that cured mental illness. The headland is a superb place for pleasant cliff walks with splendid views of Trearddur Bay to the north and Cymyran Bay to the south. At **Bwa Gwyn** (White Arch), is a memorial to Tyger, a dog that, in September 1817, led the crew of four from a sinking ketch to land. After dragging the cabin boy ashore and returning for the ship's captain the dog collapsed and died from exhaustion.

RHOSNEIGR   MAP 1 REF D3
14 miles W of Menai Bridge on A4080

This small resort is a fairly quiet spot close to sandy beaches with rocky outcrops and the nearby **Cymyran Bay**. The River Crigyll, which runs into the sea by the town, was the haunt of the 18th-century 'Wreckers of

Crigyll', who were famous for luring ships onto the rocks. Tried at Beaumaris in 1741, where the group were found guilty and hanged, the wreckers became the subject of a ballad, *The hanging of the thieves of Crigyll*. The 1,400 acres of gorse and dunes at **Tywyn Trewan Common** is a botanist and ornithologists dream.

Dating back to 1896, **The Glan-Neigr** public house was originally built as a home and surgery for an eminent doctor before it became a hotel in the 1970s and later this licensed premises. Bought in 1996 by Christine and Glyn Jones, the building was in desperate need of repair and, following a lot of hard work by the couple, The Glan-Neigr is a warm and welcoming pub that is family orientated in all respects. Open all day, every day, not only is there a fine selection of ales, beers, lagers, and ciders but Heather, the queen of the kitchen, ensures that, at both lunchtime and in the evening, customers can enjoy a delicious and tasty meal or snack.

The Glan-Neigr, Post Office Lane, Rhosneigr, Anglesey LL64 5JA
Tel: 01407 810857

Entertainment also comes high on the list at The Glan-Neigr and, as well as the live music on Saturday nights, Tuesday evening sees special low priced beer and free pool and juke box. Children are catered for too and, within the large garden, there is a safe purpose built play area. The pub also has a swinging sea angling club of which Christine and her daughter are both members.

Sandy's, High Street, Rhosneigr, Anglesey LL64 5UQ
Tel: 01407 811103

Found in the heart of Rhosneigr, is the very popular bistro and café, **Sandy's**. This family run business, owned by Sandy and Peter Bingham which they run with the able assistance of their daughter Sophie, has been in the family since 1988 but it is only recently that the successful bistro was opened. A stylish and characterful eating place, this well frequented and highly regarded café is transformed in the evening into a cosy and intimate bistro.

Combining Welsh favourites with flavours from around the world, the appetising menu is sure to offer something for everyone and it matches the same standards of good quality and service which has seen the café become one of the islanders' favourite places over the years. To add to the enjoyment of an evening meal here, for which it is best to book a table in the summer months, there is live music in the form of piano and saxophone.

Tucked away in the village of **Ty Croes**, not far from Rhosneigr, **The Queens Head** is a place well worth seeking out. Run by Julie Jones, a native of the village, this attractive public house has an olde worlde atmosphere that, along with its charming landlady, helps to make it one of the more popular places locally. Customers can enjoy their pints of well kept ale in a number of cosy areas, including the lovely snug, and there are real fires to make the atmosphere even more inviting.

Open every day and all day Friday to Sunday, this characterful and

The Queens Head, Ty Croes, near Rhosneigr, Anglesey LL63 5RW
Tel: 01407 810806

traditional pub is a welcome retreat from the rigors of modern day living and a place to come to for real friendly hospitality.

ABERFFRAW
Map 1 ref D3
11 miles W of Menai Bridge on A4080

Though this was once the capital of Gwynedd between the 7th and 13th centuries, there remains little trace of those times, though a Norman arch set in **St Beuno's Church** is said to be from the palace of the ruling Princes. However, the **Anglesey Coastal Heritage Centre** has exhibitions recounting the area's fascinating history. Inland, the **Din Dryfol Burial Chamber** is further evidence of the Iron Age life on the island.

Just to the north, on the cliff tops above Porth Trecastell, is the **Barclodiad-y-Gawres Burial Chamber**. Said to be one the finest of its kind, those wishing to visit the monument have to get the key from Beaumaris Castle whilst leaving a deposit. This attractive bay is also known as **Cable Bay**, as it was once the terminal for the Transatlantic cable.

LLANGADWALADR
Map 1 ref D3
10 miles W of Menai Bridge on A4080

This small village was reputed to be the burial ground of Welsh princes during the time that Aberffraw was Gwynedd's capital. The church here has a memorial stone to Cadfan, King of Gwynedd and the village is dedicated to Cadwaladr, Cadfan's grandson, who is thought to be the last Briton to wear the crown before the invasion of the Saxons.

Found right in the heart of Anglesey, close to the village of **Bodorgan**, to the east of Llangadwaladr, **Henblas Country Park** is one of the island's top tourist attractions and it is certainly a place that will keep all members of the family amused for hours. Owned and personally run by Lona and Elwyn Davies, this country park provides visitors with a great insight into many aspects of Welsh country life and all are encouraged to join in the

**Henblas Country Park, Bodorgan, Anglesey LL62 5DL
Tel: 01407 840440**

numerous displays and demonstrations. From falconry to sheep shearing there is something going on throughout the day. As well as the organised displays, there are tractor tours and train rides, farm animals to visit, a nature trail to follow, and a large indoor adventure playground where younger members of the family can let off some steam. There is also a café here, serving a wide range of snacks and light meals as well as liquid refreshment, and older visitors are sure to find the craft displays and the gift shop of interest. Henblas Country Park is open every day from Easter to the end of October except on non Bank Holiday Saturdays.

NEWBOROUGH   MAP 1 REF D3
8 miles SW of Menai Bridge on A4080

Founded in 1303 by former inhabitants of Llanfaes who had been removed by Edward I, the village stands on the edge of a nature reserve covering 1566 acres of dunes, coast, and forest. Among the many footpaths through the reserve, there are several forest trails that show how the Forestry Commission is constantly trying to stabilise the dunes. **Newborough Warren** is so called because, before myxomatosis, about 80,000 rabbits were trapped here annually. There is a route through the warren to **Abermenai Point** but the way is dangerous and advice concerning tidal conditions should be sought before considering the walk.

Llanddwyn Island is also accessible but again tidal conditions should be carefully studied beforehand. Until the 1920s marram grass, which was grown for conservation purposes from Elizabethan times, was also the mainstay of the area helping sustain a cottage industry in the production of ropes, baskets, matting, and thatching materials. A high embankment was built here in the 18th century by Thomas Telford to stop the sea which, before, had almost cut the island in two.

The renowned wildlife artist Charles Tunnicliffe had a studio on the island for over 30 years and Anglesey Council has purchased a collection of his marvellous work which can be seen at the Oriel Ynys Môn in Llangefni.

Southeast of Newborough lies **Anglesey Model Village and Gardens**, a delightful place where visitors can wander through the attractive landscaped gardens and see many of the island's landmarks, all built to a scale of one twelfth full size.

BRYNSIENCYN   MAP 1 REF E3
5 miles SW of Menai Bridge on A4080

Once a centre for Druid worship, sadly today no sign remains of the temple that stood at nearby **Tre-Drwy**. There are, however, several other remains of interest in the area. **Bodowyr Burial Chamber** is a massive stone seemingly delicately perched upon three uprights. The remains of **Castell Bryngwyn** and at **Caer Leb**, an earthwork consisting of a pentagonal enclosure 200 feet by 160 feet encircled by banks and ditches, are also close by.

The award winning **Anglesey Sea Zoo** takes visitors beneath the waves into the underwater world of a wide variety of sea creatures. The imaginative and innovative displays allow visitors a unique view of these interesting beasts, that include sea horses, oysters, conger eels, and rays.

Standing in its own large and secluded gardens, **Ty Coch Country Guest House** is a lovely 18th-century house which is, today, the home of Barbara and Bob Griffiths. Since the summer of 1994, this friendly couple have been offering outstanding bed and breakfast accommodation in a choice of three delightful, en-suite rooms. Well furnished and decorated, each guest room has glorious views over the southern part of the island and beyond, across the Menai Straits, to the Snowdonia mountains. Downstairs are the guest lounge, a comfortable room that is ideal for relaxing and resting in, and the dining room, which overlooks the garden and where a delicious home-cooked breakfast is served each morning.

As Barbara and Bob keep hens, amongst other animals, there are always freshly laid eggs on the table and, to further add to guests' enjoyment of the area, the couple maintain a supply of local information. They also

**Ty Coch Country Guest House, Brynsiencyn, Anglesey LL61 6SZ
Tel: 01248 430227**

run an agency that offers top class self-catering accommodation in a wide
range of houses and cottages throughout North Wales.

PLAS NEWYDD   MAP 1 REF E3
2 miles SW of Menai Bridge on A4080

Bryn-celli Ddu, a wonderful example of a Bronze Age passage grave, lies
up a narrow country road close to **Plas Newydd**, an elegant 18th-century
house that was designed by architect James Wyatt. The stately home of
the Marquis of Anglesey, the house enjoys views over the Menai Strait and
on towards Snowdonia.

There is, in the mansion, an exhibition of Rex Whistler's work, who, as
a regular guest to the house, painted a 'trompe l'oiel' decoration in the
dining room. The house also contains a **Military Museum** which holds
relics from the battle of Waterloo. Included in the displays is a boot and
the mutilated trousers worn by the first Marquis at Waterloo who, during
the battle, had an extraordinary exchange with the Duke of Wellington:

" By God Sir, I've lost my leg."
" By God, so you have."

Plas Newydd

HOLYHEAD

On the approach to Holyhead, which in fact lies on **Holy Island**, is **Penrhos Nature Reserve**, close by the aluminium factory. This location should not discourage the nature lover as the 200 acre reserve supports a variety of wildlife and contains some pleasant coastal and woodland walks.

Holyhead Mountain (Mynydd Twr) rises to 720 feet behind the town, which is the largest in Anglesey and is also a busy rail and ferry terminal for travellers to and from Ireland. Recently, to tempt more visitors, day trips to Dublin by hovercraft have been introduced. Holyhead has all the facilities needed to cater for a large community and the many who pass through its ferry terminal. A pedestrianised town centre helps make it easier and more pleasant to explore.

Parts of **St Cybi's Parish Church** date from the 14th to 17th century and it is situated within the partially surviving walls of a Roman fort on the site of the original 6th-century chapel. Nearby the church, **Egylwys Bedd** reputedly contains the tomb of Seregri, an Irish warrior who was repelled by the Welsh chief Caswallon Lawhir. The town's triumphal arches, built in 1821, commemorate George IV's visit here as well as the end of the A5, the major road from London.

There is an interesting **Maritime Museum**, open during the summer, that outlines the area's historical ties with the sea. While, the **Ucheldre Centre**, housed in a former convent chapel, is an exciting arts and exhibition centre that not only focuses on local artists and crafts people but also famous names such as Picasso and Chagall. Meanwhile, **Salt Island (Ynys Halen)** is virtually self-explanatory; a factory was built here to extract salt from seawater. Rock salt was added to improve its quality and inevitably an excise duty was charged. Smuggling flourished to **Four Mile Bridge** from the Isle of Man where salt was duty free.

South Stack Lighthouse

The **Breakwater Country Park**, just outside Holyhead, incorporates Britain's largest breakwater designed by James Meadow. Started in 1845 and taking 28 years to build, the structure shields an area of 667 acres and has a promenade running its entire length. From the country park there are many walks along the coast including routes to the North and South Stacks. Above the harbour, from the breakwater, is a memorial put there in tribute to Captain Skinner who drowned when his packet boat, *Escape*, was lost in 1832.

Views of Snowdonia, the Isle of Man, and the Mourne Mountains in Ireland are possible, on clear days, from the top of Holyhead Mountain, where evidence of ancient settlements remain. **Caer-y Twr**, an ancient fortress stands on top and another, **Cytiau'r Gwyddelod**, a hut settlement occupied in the 2nd century, is close by.

To the west of the town centre lies **South Stack** and one of Wales' most impressive lighthouses. Built in 1809, the **Lighthouse** stands on a beautiful but dangerous site that can only be reached via a steep, stone stairway of over 400 steps. However, those making the strenuous climb down (don't forget the return climb is up!) are rewarded with wonderful views of the surrounding cliff faces and the chance to observe sea birds at close quarters. In between the Stacks lies **Gogarth Bay** where there is an RSPB reserve which includes a cavern known as **Parliament House Cave** used by a profusion of sea birds; puffins, guillemots, and even falcons can be found here. **Ellin's Tower**, within the reserve, is the ideal spot for the keen ornithologist to observe the wide variety of species. The cliffs themselves are used by serious climbers for training; they are considered to be one of the most testing cliff faces in Britain.

Aqua diving, windsurfing, water skiing, and fishing are some of the many attractions in **Trearddur Bay**, a popular part of Anglesey's extensive coastline that has large, sandy beaches, clear waters, and safe bathing. Thomas Telford stayed in the Georgian house, Towyn Lodge, on the south side of the bay whilst building the A5 in the 19th century. Close by lies the **Trefignath Burial Chamber**. Consisting of a long passage once divided into several chambers, today, the east chamber is the best preserved and it is flanked by two upright stones.

Situated overlooking South Stack Lighthouse and just outside Holyhead, **South Stack Kitchen** is a superb café and restaurant that surely must have one of the most splendid outlooks in the country. Owned and personally run by David Edwards, a chef, since 1985, he has turned this small estab-

South Stack Kitchen, South Stack Road, Holyhead
Anglesey LL65 1YH Tel: 01407 762181

lishment into a wonderful café and restaurant that has an enviable reputation for its excellent food that is on offer at reasonable prices. Open every day at both lunchtime and in the evening throughout the season, the cosy and intimate restaurant serves an interesting and imaginative menu that is complemented by the wine list. A popular place, particularly with those who enjoy fine food and wine as well as an unusual location, it is preferable to book a table for dinner. For less formal dining the café, which is well frequented by walkers and climbers, serves a mouth-watering range of light meals and snacks, including a range of irresistible home-made cakes. As with the restaurant, the café is open every day from Easter to the end of October.

EAST OF HOLYHEAD

LLANFAIR-YNG-NGHORNWY   MAP 1 REF D2
7 miles E of Holyhead off A5025

This village, on the approach to **Carmel Head**, has two claims to fame. It was here that Frances Williams founded the Anglesey Association for the Preservation of Life from Shipwreck in the 19th century. With her husband, who was the local rector, she raised funds for lifeboats in Anglesey and through her efforts the first lifeboat station in the area was established. The second claim to fame is that Llanfair-yng-Nghornwy was regarded as the centre of the 'bonesetters of Anglesey', one of whom invented the splint.

The Skerries, a group of islets, lie two miles offshore from the point at Carmel Head. (Their Welsh name is Ynys-y-Moelrhoniaid, which means Island of Porpoises.) On the islets stands the last **Lighthouse** to be privately owned (ships had to pay a toll as they passed) which now has a beam capable of throwing out a 4 million candlepower light. When braziers stood there during the 18th century they burnt approximately 100 tons of coal a night!

CEMAES   MAP 1 REF D2
10 miles E of Holyhead on A5025

Cemaes Bay boasts five sheltered beaches all of which are good for swimming. Once a favourite place for smugglers and 19th-century shipping, the town is now a quiet fishing village with a small tidal harbour. Around the headland lies **Wylfa Power Station** and from its visitor centre there is not only a free guided tour of the station but a mass of information about the nature trail surrounding the plant. The pleasant well marked trail provides the opportunity to see a wide variety of plant species and wildlife. The adders, by the way, are like most wildlife - harmless if left alone and not threatened.

Ogof y March Glas - the cave of the blue horse - on Cemaes Bay was so named after an incident which happened over 200 years ago. After a family dispute, a young man furiously galloped, on his dappled blue-grey horse, away from his house near the bay. Blinded by rage he galloped headlong over a cliff. Only the young man's hat was ever found but the carcass of the horse was washed up in the cave in Cemaes Bay.

AMLWCH   MAP 1 REF E2
13 miles E of Holyhead on A5025

To the southeast of the town lies the pock marked **Parys Mountain** which has provided copper for prospectors from Roman times onwards. In 1768 a copper boom helped make Anglesey the copper centre of the world but by 1820 this rush was over - falling prices and the exhaustion of the mineral from the mountain signalled the end. Amlwch had fed off this wealth and the harbour that was built during those more prosperous times is now used mainly by pleasure craft. On Fridays there is a lively market in the town which might interest the visitor.

The Liverpool Arms is now only one of two remaining pubs of the original 54 that used to offer refreshment to the locals and seafarers in Amlwch's heyday as a port. Dating back to the early 1800s, this charming pub is personally run by Gaynor Washington-Jones with the very able assistance of her husband, Phil. A place full of character, as befits a building of this age, The Liverpool Arms not only has a nautical feel but the walls are adorned with pictures of Gaynor's family and friends. As well as the cosy bar, with its fine selection of ales, beers, and lagers, there is also a small and intimate restaurant to the rear and, outside, an attractive beer garden.

The Liverpool Arms, Machine Street, Amlwch Port
Anglesey LL68 9HA Tel: 01407 830671

A wide range of bar snacks are served throughout the premises to complement the more formal dining of the restaurant. Gaynor is the chef of the partnership and this popular restaurant has gained a large following on the island and it is advisable to book a table, particularly at the weekends. With fine food and drink and the superb friendly atmosphere The Liverpool Arms is certainly a pub well worth visiting and, for those interested in entertainment, Gaynor and Phil also hold Kareoke nights on Thursdays and Fridays and there is live music on Saturday evenings.

DULAS
MAP 1 REF E2
14 miles E of Holyhead on A5025

This once thriving village had, in the early 19th century, a brickworks and a shipbuilding industry. Standing at the head of the Dulas River which runs into the bay, from here and the rocky headland further north, **Ynys Dulas** a small island that is the haunt of grey seals, can be seen. On the island itself is a 19th-century tower built as a beacon and refuge for sailors and the lady of Llysdulas manor house once had food left there for stranded mariners. Around the headland lies **Traeth-yr-ora**, a secluded sandy beach that is almost landlocked and is a birdwatchers paradise as many breeds nest here.

LLANERCH-Y-MEDD
MAP 1 REF D2
11 miles E of Holyhead on B5111

To the north lies **Llyn Alaw**, the island's largest lake that is also well stocked with both rainbow and brown trout. A great place for fishermen, the lakeside is popular as a picnic spot and with those searching out Anglesey's bird and plant life. Covering some 770 acres, the lake is actually man-made from the flooding of marshland, and it supplies most of the island's industrial and domestic needs.

Found in a quiet rural location, very much off the beaten track, **Mynydd Mwyn Mawr** is a charming farmhouse at the centre of a 400 acre working mixed beef and sheep farm. The home of Sarah and John Astley, from

**Mynydd Mwyn Mawr, Llanerch-y-medd, Anglesey LL71 7AG
Tel: 01248 470276**

their delightful turn of the century house they offer comfortable and re-laxing bed and breakfast accommodation in a choice of three cosy rooms. Each has glorious views over the mid-Anglesey countryside and are just the place to come back to after a day out exploring the island. Breakfast is served each morning in the dining room and whilst there are no evening meals, packed lunches are provided by prior arrangement. A place for all the family, Mynydd Mwyn Mawr is very much a working farm and guests are welcome to participate in the farming activities where it is safe to do so. There is also a large, enclosed garden that is ideal for children and the Astley's dogs, Spot, Moi, and Floss are always on hand ready to be enter-tained.

LLANDDEUSANT
6 miles E of Holyhead off A5025

MAP 1 REF D2

The village is home to Anglesey's only stone tower working windmill that

was built in 1775. Now fully re-stored, **Llynnon Mill** is open to the public and not only can the mill's stoneground flour be purchased here but there is also an attractive craftshop and a popular tea rooms.

Tradition has it that the green mound **Bedd Branwen**, near the River Alaw, is the grave of Branwen, the heroine of the 14th-century Welsh epic *Mabinogion*. Opened in 1813, a rough-baked clay urn con-taining fragments of burnt bone and ashes was found here. Since the dis-covery, in 1967, of more funeral urns the site has become more significant.

Found in a charming and un-spoilt part of the island at **Llanfachraeth** to the west of Llanddeusant, **Penyrorsedd Farm**, has been in Joyce Roberts' family for

Llynnon Mill, Llanddeusant

many years and she and her husband, Emlyn, are the third generation at this 400 acre beef and sheep farm. At its centre is the delightful early 18th-century farmhouse from where Joyce also offers outstanding bed and breakfast accommodation in a choice of two comfortable guest rooms. Well decorated and furnished, as is the rest of the house, the rooms not only have splendid views over the north of the island but guests will also find little extras that make Penyrorsedd Farm a real home from home.

**Penyrorsedd Farm, Llanfachraeth, near Holyhead
Anglesey LL65 4YB Tel: 01407 730630**

Downstairs, leading off from the hall with its beautiful Victorian tiled floor, there is a guest lounge that is the perfect place to relax after a day out exploring Anglesey. Breakfast, served in the separate dining room, is a real feast and as well as using only the finest local produce the free range eggs come fresh from the farm. Joyce's culinary skills do not end there as, on arrival, guests are not only treated to a warm and friendly welcome but also have the opportunity to sample some of her home-made cakes and scones. Penyrorsedd Farm is certainly an ideal spot from which to discover Anglesey and it makes the ideal family holiday base.

At **Llanfwrog**, to the west of Llanddeusant, and enjoying a peaceful setting adjacent to Porth Tywyn-mawr, with its beautiful beach, the aptly named **Sandy Beach Caravan Park** is the ideal place to relax and get away from the hustle and bustle of daily life. Set in 15 acres of lovely Welsh

**Sandy Beach Caravan Park, Porth Tywyn-mawr, Llanfwrog
Anglesey LL65 4YH Tel: 01407 730302**

countryside, the site has 82 static caravans, of which five are for hire, providing very well-equipped holiday accommodation with all the facilities anyone could need. There are also pitches for 40 touring caravans, as well as a camping area of three acres situated right next to the beach. To complete their stay, holidaymakers will find the site offers first class amenities which include toilets and showers, a site shop, laundry, telephone, chemical disposal, electric hook-up points, and a children's play area. The owners have also added a café and restaurant to the Park.

VALLEY   Map 1 ref D3
3 miles E of Holyhead on A5

The village was thought to have gained its name when Thomas Telford was cutting his road through a small hill here. Centuries earlier this was the home of Iron Age man whose weapons and horse trappings found in the area are now on display in the National Museum of Wales.

Valley, however, is perhaps better known today for the nearby airfield established in 1941 as a fighter pilot base. In 1943 the American Airforce expanded the base's capability for use as an Atlantic terminal for arriving US military and now the RAF use the base for training flights and Air/Sea rescue. Before the bridges to Holyhead were built during the construction of the A5, the crossing to the town was made via **Pont Rhyd Bont**, now called Four Mile Bridge.

5 Vale of Clwyd and East Conwy

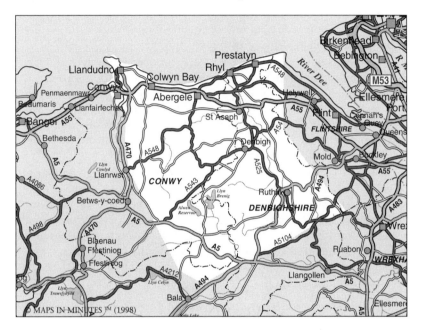

© MAPS IN MINUTES ™ (1998)

Apart from the holiday resorts along the coast, this area of Wales is often overlooked as visitors make their way to the delights of Snowdonia National Park further west. However, this very traditional region, where Welsh is often still spoken on a daily basis, has many treasures, both man-made and natural, to discover.

The coastline, from Llandudno to Prestatyn, was, before the coming of the railways, littered with small fishing villages. During the 19th century, as the hours of the millworkers from the industrial towns of Lancashire and others tied up in the factories of the Midlands were reduced, the concept of an annual holiday beside the sea grew. Served by a newly built railway network, the fishing villages expanded to accommodate the visitors and, not only were boarding houses and hotels built, but amusements became a regular feature. Less popular today, now that air travel is well within the reach of most people, many of the resorts have suffered from a lack of trade. Llandudno, always considered a 'cut above' still retains much of its Victorian and Edwardian charm, whilst other resorts, such as Rhyl, has endeavoured to counter the unsettled British summer weather by the creation of an indoor 'sun and sea' complex.

The coastline is not without its history and Prestatyn, to the east, lies at one end of Offa's Dyke. Built more as a line of demarcation rather than as a fortification, the dyke runs from the coast southwards to Cheptow. Still substantially marking the border - the placenames to the east are English and to the west Welsh - many sections of the dyke are visible and a waymarked path covers its 167 mile length. The footpath was opened in 1971 by the Countryside Commission and, running the full length, it travels through farmland as well as crossing less hospitable countryside.

The origins of this great earthwork are shrouded in mystery, though it is commonly accepted that its construction was due to the efforts of Offa, the powerful King of Mercia in the 8th century. No documentation exists and archaeologists have interpreted the design and purpose from what can be seen today. Never a continuous dyke, the earthwork took advantage of natural barriers, such as forests, in its construction and Offa's Dyke marked the western boundary of the Kingdom of Mercia.

Behind the coast lie the ancient market towns of Denbigh and Ruthin which were both home to castles built by Edward I. Attractive places to visit, they still serve the needs of the farmers of the fertile Vale of Clwyd. In this picturesque and gentle countryside can also be found Britain's smallest cathedral at St Asaph. As with many of the towns and villages of the area, the town and its cathedral have had a stormy history: first coming under attack during Edward I's conquest of the region in the 13th century and again during Owain Glyndwr's subsequent rebellion.

LLANDUDNO

Originally just a collection of fishermen's cottages, Llandudno, the 'Queen of Welsh Resorts', was developed in the 1850s under the watchful eye of the Liverpool surveyor Owen Williams who planned the resort's pleasant layout of wide streets and the Promenade. The roots of the town, however, can be found on Great Orme, just to the north of the town centre. The home of Bronze Age miners, then the Romans, in the 6th century St Tudno chose Great Orme as the site of the cell from which he preached - the town's name means the Holy Enclosure of St Tudno. The parish church built here, dedicated to St Tudno, dates back probably to the 12th century. **Llandudno Museum** describes the town's fascinating history, from its earliest days through to modern times, with a series of interesting displays and exhibits.

Great Orme's Head rises to dominate and divide the Llandudno's two beaches and is a place of great interest. Two miles long, one mile wide, and 679 feet high, its name, Orme, is thought to have originated from an old Norse word for sea monster. Now a country park, its attractions also include gardens, copper mines dating from prehistoric times, and a dry ski slope. The summit can be reached by a tramway, constructed in 1902, coach or cable car, its 520 feet making it the longest in Britain. Beneath Great Orme is an ornate pier, lying at the end of a long, gently curving promenade.

Away from the Orme the town itself is a delightful example of Victorian architecture. The **Promenade** is lined with renovated, redecorated elegant looking hotels and the wide boulevard gives it an air of the French Riviera. Its architectural renaissance has not damaged the air of fading refinement which adds a certain charm and innocence to the resort. Lewis Carroll's *Alice in Wonderland* is said to have been inspired by a friend's daughter's holiday in the resort. A **Visitor Centre** at the Rabbit Hole in Trinity Square tells the story of Alice. Further along, in Bodhyfryd Road, is **Childhood Revisited**, which houses, amongst other things, a fascinating collection of dolls, playthings, games, and British motorcycles from days gone by. A permanent Punch and Judy show can be watched on the promenade close by the pier and Prince Edward Square. The Suffragettes attempted to burn this pier in 1914 during their fight for the right of women to vote and Ringo Starr, of Beatle fame, once worked on the pleasure steamers that docked by Llandudno pier unaware that a few years later his life was to radically change.

Llandudno lays claim to being the largest seaside resort in Wales. A walk along the unspoilt promenade reveals a continuous façade of Victorian history and character.

Just south of Llandudno, **Deganwy** shares the same stretch of coastline and, though it was once a thriving fishing village, it has been taken over by its larger neighbour. Often mentioned in Welsh history, Deganwy, which means 'the fort on the Conwy', was a strategically important stronghold and its castle was the seat of Maelgwn Gwynedd as early as the 6th century. The first medieval castle was probably built here by Lupus, Earl of Chester, shortly after the Norman Conquest. The remains seen today are, however, of a castle built by one of the Earl's successors in 1211. Henry II was besieged here by the Welsh and Deganwy was finally destroyed by Llewelyn the Last in 1263.

Owned and personally run by Jacquie and Stephen Rawicki, **Number 1's Bistro**, in the oldest part of the town, has an enviable reputation for the high standard of its excellent cuisine. Housed in a building that is reputed to be Llandudno's oldest and which was once part of the Mostyn Estate Office, this attractive and stylish restaurant is well decorated and furnished to create an atmosphere of intimacy.

Open for lunch from Tuesday to Saturday and every evening but Sunday, this popular place is renowned for its interesting and enticing menus that change regularly. Stephen is the chef of the partnership and he combines the very best of local fresh ingredients in an imaginative manner and many of the dishes come with a delicious sauce. It is these sauces that

Number 1's Bistro, 1 Old Road, Llandudno, Conwy LL30 2HA
Tel & Fax: 01492 875424

are not only the house speciality but also upon which the bistro's reputation is founded. Delicate or spicy they enhance the main dish and provide another dimension to the splendid cuisine. Number 1's fish menu is also highly regarded and varies daily depending on the local availability. With Jacquie looking after the guests and managing the wine, a meal at this delightful restaurant is a treat that is certainly not to be missed.

Situated close to the town's amenities and only a short walk from the promenade, pier, and beaches, **Epperstone Hotel** is ideally placed for a short break or a family holiday in this splendid resort. Built over 100 years ago, this large detached hotel has spacious well proportioned Victorian rooms and features many of the house's original fixtures including a grand mahogany staircase, stained glass, and several superb fireplaces. However, Epperstone Hotel's most attractive aspect must be the elegant Edwardian blue lounge, a haven of peace and tranquillity and there is also a Victorian-style conservatory overlooking the well tended garden.

Owned and personally run by David Drew since 1985, this comfortable and attractive hotel offers the very best in friendly, courteous hospitality. There are eight charming en-suite guest rooms, one of which

**Epperstone Hotel, 15 Abbey Road, Llandudno, Gwynedd LL30 2EE
Tel: 01492 878746 Fax: 01492 871223**

is on the ground floor, and a full range of range of holiday packages and special activity breaks are provided. David is ably helped in the running of the establishment by his son, Stephen, the chef of the partnership. Preparing an interesting and imaginative menu of dishes, dinner in the intimate and pleasant dining room is an excellent way to end the day.

Situated close to the railway line in **Llandudno Junction,** just south of the main resort, **The Maelgwyn** is a popular place frequented by both locals and visitors who appreciate the warm and friendly atmosphere of

**The Maelgwyn, Kimberley Terrace, Llandudno Junction, Conwy
LL31 9EE Tel: 01492 582789**

this public house. Owned and personally run by Bethan and Tony Roberts, Hefin Jones, and chef Alan Stewart, these four partners have certainly made this the place for good food, drink, and company in the town. Spacious and well decorated and furnished inside, the pub not only serves an excellent range of beers and ales but also a tasty menu of quality food for which Alan is renowned. A great place for all the family, there is a separate children's room, those interested in sport and entertainment will certainly enjoy a visit here. Not only is satellite sport available on a large screen television but the pub has several ladies' and men's darts and pool teams and there is a quiz and disco each Thursday evening.

EAST OF LLANDUDNO

RHOS ON SEA   MAP 2 REF G2
4 miles E of Llandudno on B5115

This very sedate north Wales coast resort has a breakwater to shelter the small, pleasure boats and, along the promenade, is the small **Chapel of St Trillo**. It stands on the spot reputed to be where Owain Gwynedd set sail, in 1170, to eventually set foot on the North American continent, 322 years before Columbus made his discovery! The chapel is the only surviving building of an abbey that was here in the 12th century. Also on the waterfront is the **Harlequin Puppet Theatre**, Britain's only purpose-built puppet theatre.

COLWYN BAY   MAP 2 REF G3
6 miles E of Llandudno on A55

A more genteel place than the resorts found to the east, Colwyn Bay was built largely during the last century to fill the gap along the North Wales coast between Llandrillo-yn-Rhos and the village of Old Colwyn. As a result, there are many fine examples of Victorian architecture to be seen here. The beach is also served by a length of promenade with many attractions found along this thoroughfare. **Eirias Park** has plenty to offer visitors of all ages, including a Leisure Centre, **Dinosaur World** (home to the largest collection of these creatures in Britain), and picnic and adventure areas.

Colwyn Bay is also home to the very popular **Welsh Mountain Zoo** where feeding the sea lions attracts many onlookers. Perhaps more impressive is the regular free-flying displays of their collection of eagles and other birds of prey. The Zoo is deeply involved in a breeding programme for endangered species, including the American Bald Eagle, the Persian Leopard, and the Mongolian Wild Horse.

ABERGELE   MAP 2 REF H3
10 miles E of Llandudno on A55

Along with **Pensarn**, its neighbour, Abergele forms a popular joint resort which is more modest than places such as Rhyl, Prestatyn, and Colwyn Bay. Outside the town, on Tower Hill, is a mock Norman castle, **Gwrych**, built in 1814 and formerly the seat of the Earl of Dundonald. It is now a holiday centre and amongst its many attractions are medieval jousts and banquets. Behind and higher up are the natural caverns of **Cefn-Yr-Ogo** where, from the summit, there are magnificent views of the surrounding coast line to be had.

Found on the main street, **The Tuck Shop** is just the place for those who enjoy real home-cooking. As well as being a grocers shop, owned and

personally run by Les Parkinson, with the help of his sister Sally and mother Mary, this is also an excellent café. Open from 07.30 to 17.00 during the week and until 14.00 on Saturday's, the café serves a wide range of meals and snacks as well as a superb breakfast. Everything is freshly prepared, including the mouth-watering sandwich fillings, and the delicious cakes, fruit tarts, and pastries on display in the window are baked at home by Mary and brought to the shop each day. Not surprisingly, this is a

The Tuck Shop, 3 Rhuddlan Road, Abergele,
Conwy LL22 7HH Tel: 01745 826346

popular haunt for locals and visitors lucky enough to find the shop are really in for a treat.

RHUDDLAN   MAP 2 REF H3
15 miles E of Llandudno on A525

The site of an early Welsh stronghold, **Twt Hill**, Rhuddlan is now overshadowed by its impressive castle ruins. Sometimes referred to as the 'Cradle of Wales' it was here that Edward I, using **Rhuddlan Castle** as his headquarters during his campaign, issued the Statute of Rhuddlan that united the Principality of Wales to the Kingdom of England and gave the town a Royal Charter when his sovereignty was confirmed in 1284. The statute was enacted on the site now occupied by Parliament House, on Parliament Street, and there is a commemoration tablet on the wall that is said to be from the original building. Like other castles in the area Rhuddlan was partially destroyed during the Civil War.

Though the town does not lie on the coast, at this point the River Clwyd is still tidal and, as a result, Rhuddlan was not only a strategic position to be held but also had a port. **Gillot's Tower**, by the dockgate, was built by James of St George, who was also responsible for an interesting concentric plan which allowed arches on inner and outer walls to fire at the same time.

Close by is the attractive late 17th-century **Bodryhddan Hall**, home to the ancestors of Lord Langford. As well as being home to the Charter of Rhuddlan, visitors can also see, in the white drawing room (around the fireplaces), panels which came from the chapel of a ship of the Spanish Aramda that floundered off the coast of Anglesey.

Found in Rhuddlan's main street, **The King's Head**, run by Sam and Kevin Birtles, was built earlier this century on the site of a previous inn. As well as the pub area, which serves real ales in a warm and friendly atmosphere that is livened up regularly by live music, the main area of interest is the newly refurbished restaurant. Taking the theme of Old Rhuddlan for the extensive redecoration, the restaurant is a tribute to the pride that the local community has for its town and history. The town's two treasured sites: St Mary's Church and the Castle are featured on the restaurant's main doors as well as a portrait of Edward I, who established his parliament in Rhuddlan in 1283. Across the doors and windows is the crossed pattern of the Celtic Friendship Knot, which not only signifies the

The King's Head, High Street, Rhuddlan, Denbighshire LL18 2TU
Tel: 01745 590345

warm welcome found here but throughout the town. In these extremely interesting and pleasant surroundings, both a lunchtime and an evening menu are served which have been compiled by Sam. Those who have worked up an appetite early can also take advantage of the mouth-watering breakfast menu that is served between 09.30 and 11.30.

RHYL   MAP 2 REF H2
14 miles E of Llandudno on A458

Little more than a couple of fishermen's cottages until its development as a holiday resort in 1833, Rhyl was, before easy and cheap air travel, the destination for many workers and their families from the industrial towns and cities of Wales, the Midlands, and the northwest looking for a break on the north Wales coast.

Though the heyday of this once elegant resort has long since passed, Rhyl still has a lot to offer the holidaymaker of today. As well as the full range of amusement arcades and seaside attractions, it is home to two large and exciting attractions: the **Sun Centre**, one of the first all-weather leisure complexes, and **Sea Life**, where an exciting journey of discovery beneath the waves is promised to all.

Situated opposite Rhyl's popular Children's Village is another attraction well worthy of a visit; **Robin's Corner Café**. Hard to miss, this large white-painted premises is owned and personally run by Michelle and Dave Taylor, with the help of Dave's mother June. Open all day, every day,

Robin's Corner Café, 14-15 West Parade, Rhyl
Denbighshire LL18 1HE Tel: 01745 353484

during the season, until 22.30 (until 17.00 in winter), this is a popular place for a meal at any time. The extensive menu covers all the usual favourites and includes the substantial all day breakfast as well as the less expected curries and chillies. Children too will enjoy their menu, with the addition of a free toy.

DYSERTH   MAP 2 REF I3
17 miles E of Llandudno on A5151

Lying in the foothills of the Clwydian Range and below Graig Fawr's slopes, the village is home to a 60 foot waterfall as well as a charming parish church dating from the 13th century.

Visiting the nearby village of **Cwm** and **The Blue Lion Inn** and Chambers Restaurant, the finest 16th-century freehouse in North Wales, is like taking a step back in time. Famous for its collection of over 200 chamber pots hanging from the oak beamed ceilings, the warm welcome is increased on those chilly nights by the real fires in the inglenook fireplaces. Food is

The Blue Lion Inn, Cwm, Dyserth, near Rhyl
Denbighshire LL18 5SG Tel: 01745 570733 Fax: 01745 571987

the main priority at The Blue Lion, which is owned by Peggy and Terry Williams, with their son Mark as Head Chef. The impressive Chambers Restaurant offers a high standard of cuisine with a choice of table d'hôte, an imaginative à la carte menu, and superb Sunday lunch. The popular bistro carvery food bar offers informal lunchtime and evening meals with chef's daily blackboard specials complemented by the unique help your-self salad bar. The inn's tranquil situation in the beautiful Vale of Clwyd overlooking the Snowdonian range, makes The Blue Lion the ideal desti-nation for walkers with its close proximity to Offa's Dyke. For the less energetic and anyone who enjoys good views and peace and quiet in lovely surroundings, The Blue Lion is the place to visit.

PRESTATYN   Map 2 ref 12
17 miles E of Llandudno on A458

With three miles or so of sandy beaches Prestatyn has proved a popular
holiday destination over the years and, as expected, there are all types of
entertainment available making the town an ideal centre for family holidays.

There is little to keep the historically curious satisfied but the **Offa's
Dyke Centre** is worth the visit. Prestatyn lies at the start, or end, of this
170 mile footpath that follows the line of the ancient earthwork to
Chepstow. As well as a fine diagram of the whole walk, there are also
numerous leaflets and booklets about the path.

DENBIGH

Though not as important a town as it once was, Denbigh still retains a
charm that is enhanced by buildings dating from the 16th century onwards and most of the centre of this old market town is now a conservation
area. The old town was concentrated around the castle which was built
on the site of a Roman settlement and commands good views over the
Vale of Clwyd.

Denbigh Castle ruins are an impressive sight and the fortress was,
before Edward I's conquest of Wales, the stronghold of the Welsh prince
Dafydd ap Gruffyd, brother of Llewelyn the Last. Henry de Lacy, Earl of
Lincoln was given the Lordship of Denbigh by Edward and building was
started on the 'new' castle in 1282. The walled town was completed by
1311 but it was subject to sporadic attacks during its occupation. In 1402,
Owain Glyndwr laid siege to Denbigh during his rebellion and, in the War

of the Roses, the old
town was burnt to the
ground and it gradually
moved down from the
hilltop to its present
market place position.
During the Civil War,
Charles I stayed at the
castle in 1645 which
later endured a six
month siege before fall-
ing, in October 1646, to
Parliament forces.

Gradually Denbigh
developed around the
market place and town

The Burgess Gate, Denbigh Castle

square and, nowadays, this is where the most interesting buildings can be found. The narrow thoroughfares of Vale and High Streets enhance the olde worlde feel of this compact town.

Denbigh has many famous sons, too many to list here, including: Thomas Edwards (Twm o'r Nant), an actor and playwright who is buried in Denbigh's oldest church, St Marcella's; and Thomas Gee, a printer and publisher of the Welsh language. The paper he originated *Baner ac Amserau Cymru* is still published today. Famous visitors to the town have included, amongst others, Dr Samuel Johnson and Beatrix Potter.

Found near the centre of Denbigh, **The Hope and Anchor** is an outstanding pub that dates back to the 16th century and was, originally, a coaching inn serving the needs of weary travellers. Though times have certainly changed, landlord and lady, John and Marilyn Cooke still believe

The Hope and Anchor, 94 Vale Street, Denbigh
Denbighshire LL16 3BW Tel: 01745 815115

in offering customers great hospitality with good food and drink and comfortable accommodation. The pub is open every day, all day Friday to Sunday, and there is a fine selection of ales, beers, and lagers from the bar. In these traditional surroundings, customers can also enjoy a delicious meal in the charming restaurant area in the evening. Entertainment is also on the menu here as not only is there a quiz night each Thursday evening, but to the rear of the premises there is a safe children's play area, a delightful beer garden, and a boules pitch. Those looking for accommodation in the town will also be able to take advantage of the four comfortable and well furnished guest rooms above the inn.

NORTH OF DENBIGH

BODELWYDDAN
MAP 2 REF H3
7 miles N of Denbigh off A55

The village church, known as the **Marble Church**, was built in 1856-60 by Lady Willoughby de Broke as a memorial to her husband. The landmark white spire is of local limestone, whilst inside there is an arcade of marble.

Opposite the eye-catching church stands **Bodelwyddan Castle**, a Victorian building which contains a collection of some 200 paintings on permanent loan from the National Portrait Gallery. Though built in the

Bodelwyddan Castle

19th century, the castle occupies the site of a 15th-century house. Exhibitions are often held in the Williams Hall, which is authentically refurbished, again in Victorian style, and there are attractive gardens to wander around. Occasionally a fireworks and laser display combined with a symphony concert are put on in the grounds.

ST ASAPH
MAP 2 REF I3
5 miles N of Denbigh on A525

This small town, on a ridge between the Rivers Clwyd and Elwy, ranks as a city because of its cathedral. Standing on a hill, Britain's smallest cathedral has had a particularly stormy history. Originally founded in AD 560 by St Kentigern (also known as St Mungo), it was sacked by Henry III's forces in 1245, then destroyed during Edward I's conquest some 37 years later. Edward I wished to rebuild at Rhuddlan, but Bishop Anian II insisted that the new cathedral be at St Asaph and so the building standing

St Asaph's Cathedral

today was started by Anian and completed by his two successors. In 1402, the woodwork was burnt during Owain Glyndwr's rebellion and subsequently restored by Bishop Redman. Finally, the tower was rebuilt in 1715 after it had been destroyed in a storm! **St Asaph's Cathedral** holds several treasures such as the Celestory Windows (1403) and a first edition William Morgan Bible from 1588 in Welsh that was used at the 1969 Investiture of the Prince of Wales. A Welsh-born preacher, Morgan set about his translation of the Bible into Welsh so that this work, and not the English version, could be used in Welsh services. Working away in Llanrhaeadr ym Mochnant and taking around 25 years to complete, Morgan became so engrossed in his task that his parishioners became upset at his neglect of duty and he had to be escorted by armed guards to the church. Not only was the finished work important to the Welsh churches, each one of which received a copy of the translation, but it also set a standard for the Welsh language, which, without being codified could have been lost forever.

St Asaph was Bishop of the Cathedral during the 6th century and a particularly fishy legend is connected with him. One day, Nest, the wife of Maelgwn Gwynedd, King of North Wales, lost a precious ring whilst she was bathing in a pool. Given to her by Maelgwn, this ring was traditionally worn by the Queens of the North and she went to see St Asaph hoping that he might help her to retrieve the ring. The bishop invited the royal couple to dine with him the following evening. The next night St Asaph told Maelgwn about the loss of ring and the king became angry. Before they sat down to eat, St Asaph prayed for its safe return. The meal began with fish caught in the nearby River Elwy and, when Maelgwn cut into his fish, the ring fell out on his plate!

TREMEIRCHION
MAP 2 REF I3

4 miles N of Denbigh off A55

This small village is home to several buildings of interest. The 13th-century village church houses a 14th-century tomb-niche containing the effigy of a vested priest. In the chancel, a tablet commemorates Hester Lynch Piozzi who was better known as Dr Johnston's Mrs Thrale.

In 1567, Sir Richard Clough, a wealthy merchant, built a house, Bachegraig, near Tremeirchion. Though now demolished, the gatehouse still stands. Its unusual architectural style so shocked the local inhabitants that they thought the Devil must have been the architect and had also supplied the bricks. The local story has it that the Devil baked the bricks in the fires of Hell and, to this day, a nearby stream is known as Nant y Cythraul, the Devil's Brook.

BODFARI
MAP 2 REF I3

3 miles NE of Denbigh off A543

Found in the heart of the Vale of Clwyd at the foot of the Clwydian Range, Bodfari marks the abrupt change in the landscape from arable fields to heath and moorland. From here the River Clwyd meanders gently down towards Rhyl and the sea, whilst the Offa's Dyke Path passes close by.

The Downing Arms, a charming 16th-century building, is named after Lord Downing, who once owned the estate in which the village of Bodfari stood. Managed by a mother and son team, Marjorie and Kevin

The Downing Arms, Mold Road, Bodfari, Denbighshire LL16 4DW
Tel: 01745 710265

Turner, this lovely pub is open every day and all day at the weekends and
on Bank Holidays. The perfect place to come to for those who enjoy an
excellent pint of real ale, the pub also has an enviable reputation for the
fine food that is served at both lunchtime and in the evenings. In the
comfortable and cosy surroundings of the quaint old inn, and beneath the
collection of tea cups hanging from the beams, customers can choose their
meal from the extensive menu and the supplementary list of daily specials. Ranging from light snacks and meals to full à la carte dinners, the
menus cater for all tastes and certainly go far beyond the normal pub
food. Very popular for both Saturday evening and Sunday lunch, when
booking is preferred, the monthly themed menu events, on Fridays, are
well worth attending and, over the year, they take customers on a trip
around the world. Children are not forgotten at The Downing Arms either and, outside, there is a large, safe play area, adjacent to the attractive
patio-style beer garden.

WEST OF DENBIGH

LLANFAIR TALHAIARN	MAP 2 REF H3

8 miles W of Denbigh on A544

This village is the burial place of John Jones (1810-1869), a poet who was
acclaimed as the Welsh Burns.

   Nestling in the heart of this picturesque village and adjacent to the
River Elwy is the magnificent **Black Lion Hotel**. Dating back to the mid
19th century, this charming and welcoming establishment is owned and
personally run by Gareth Edwards and his family. Renowned for the high
quality of its food and drink, along with its superb hospitality, The Black
Lion Hotel is a very popular place and well frequented by the locals. The

The Black Lion Hotel, Llanfair Talhaiarn, Denbighshire LL22 8RY
Tel: 01745 720205 Fax: 01745 720223

cosy bar, a great meeting place for those living in the village, is a lively place on Fridays, when there is usually live music. This is the place to come to for an excellent pint of real ale and a range of delicious bar snacks and meals. For more formal dining, the hotel's restaurant has a superb à la carte menu of traditionally based home-cooked dishes that make use of the very best of Welsh produce. Add to this the well chosen wine list and dining here is a treat not to be missed. Finally, The Black Lion Hotel also offers customers the opportunity of an peaceful night's sleep in one of their spacious and comfortable guest rooms.

LLANGERNYW   MAP 2 REF G3
11 miles W of Denbigh on A548

This quiet Denbighshire village was the birthplace of Sir Henry Jones, in 1852, who went on to become known as the cobbler philosopher. The son of the local shoemaker, Henry Jones was apprenticed to his father at the age of 12 but, despite inadequate education and poverty, he managed to qualify as a teacher before winning a scholarship to study philosophy at Glasgow University. His academic career flourished and, as well as becoming a highly acclaimed lecturer greatly interested in social affairs and liberalism, he was finally awarded a knighthood in 1912. Though Sir Henry Jones is buried in Glasgow, this village has not forgotten its local hero. In 1934, Jones' childhood home was purchased by a fund set up to honour his memory and work. Today, with the help of a Heritage Lottery Fund grant, the **Sir Henry Jones Museum** has been able to re-open the museum and conserve many of the artefacts found here. The new displays include a reconstruction of the shoemaker's workshop and the rest of the cottage provides an insight into the lives of many living in Llangernyw at the time of Jones' childhood.

However, the museum is not the only attraction this village has to offer as, in the churchyard of St Digain's Church lies the Llangernyw Yew. The oldest known tree in Wales, and one of the oldest living things in the world, the yew is estimated to be over 4,000 year old.

Set in this beautiful village is one of the finest pubs in the area, **The Stag**. Owned and personally run by Adam and Jo Barlow, with the help of their daughter, Harriet, this 16th-century property is steeped in history. Every nook and cranny is home to a magnificent collection of memorabilia, from over 30 chiming clocks to a large stuffed alligator and a selection of army hats! A real hidden treasure, The Stag not only serves a selection of at least four real ales at any one time, but there is also a comprehensive menu of tasty bar snacks and meals. As well as the more usual dishes, guests can sample more exotic flavours that come from the four corners of the globe - the British beef steaks are a particular feature and practically form a menu in themselves. With delicious food, fine wines, and plenty

**The Stag, Llangernyw, near Abergele, Conwy LL22 8PP
Tel: 01745 860213**

of real ale, The Stag certainly has a lot to offer its customers and, for those who wish to stay a while, there are also three cosy and very comfortable guest rooms available all year round.

SOUTH OF DENBIGH

RUTHIN   MAP 4 REF I4
6 miles SE of Denbigh on A525

This old market town lies in the Vale of Clwyd, more or less surrounded by a ring of hills, and the town's layout appears to have changed little from medieval days. St Peter's Square is a good place from which to view the town and, in particular, its impressive, landmark church. **St Peter's Church**, its fairly modern spire rising from its position tucked away in a corner, was founded in 1310 as a collegiate church. Inside, the church's early 16th-century oak roof consists of 408 panels and the cloisters attached to the church date from the 14th century. In the grounds is Christ's Hospital, founded in 1590, with its collection of picturesque almshouses.

St Peter's Square itself is edged by many lovely buildings. The 15th-century Myddelton Arms is particularly eyecatching because of its unusual Dutch architectural style and seven dormer windows dubbed as the 'eyes of Ruthin', whilst the adjacent hotel is a fine example of Georgian architecture. Cock fights were once held in a pit at the back of the premises. On the southside of the square, the **Old Courthouse**, a renovated timber and wattle building dating from 1401, is now home to a bank. Down Castle Street amongst many fine buildings is one of Wales' finest examples of an Elizabethan town house, **Nant Clwyd House**.

Ruthin Castle, begun in 1277 by Edward I, was the home of Lord de Grey of Ruthin who, having proclaimed Owain Glyndwr a traitor to Henry IV, was given a large area of land originally held by the Welshman. After Glyndwr crowned himself Prince of Wales, de Grey was the first to suffer when Ruthin was attacked in 1400. Though the town was all but destroyed, the castle held out and survived the onslaught. During the Civil War, the castle again came under siege, this time surviving for 11 weeks before eventually falling to General Mytton in 1646, who had the building destroyed. Today's castle is a partial restoration of the original building and is a hotel specialising in medieval banquets.

Nant Clwyd House, Ruthin

The Town Hall, on Market Street, is another fine example of period architecture, this time Victorian. The town is also renowned for **Maen Huail,** a stone which also stands in the market place. According to legend, Huail was beheaded on this stone by King Arthur because of rivalrous love.

Found right in the heart of Ruthin is the impressive **Castle Hotel,** an attractive and imposing red brick building that dates back to the 18th century. This family run establishment offers everything that visitors to this popular town could wish for when staying away from home. The charming and pleasant owners, Janet and Roy Hughes, aided by their two young daughters, Lili and Ruby, offer comfortable accommodation in a choice of 15 en-suite guest rooms, with either views over the town's St

Peter's Square or over the rolling hills behind the town.

Adjacent to the hotel is the Myddelton Arms, also owned by the family, in another attractive building which, this time, dates from the 15th century. Here, not only is there an excellent pub on the ground floor, which serves bar meals as well as a well put together list of ales, but on the first floor is the hotel's restaurant. Open to non-residents, this is a popular and well regarded restaurant that serves a tasty menu of light lunches with a fine evening à la carte menu that is supplemented by the chef's daily specials list. Booking is advisable on Friday and Saturday evenings for non-residents whilst those staying at the Castle Hotel can also make their choice of dish from the well selected table d'hôte menu.

The Castle Hotel, St Peter's Square, Ruthin, Denbighshire LL15 1AA
Tel: 01824 702479/705824 Fax: 01824 703488

Finally, the Hughes family also have a night club in Ruthin, The Venue, that is open on both Friday and Saturday evenings - ideal for those who enjoy dancing the night away.

Dating back to 1636, **The Star** is an outstanding family run pub that should not be missed. An attractive white building abundantly decorated

The Star, 55 Clwyd Street, Ruthin, Denbighshire LL15 1HH
Tel: 01824 703614

with hanging baskets and window boxes in the summer, David and Diane Thomas, with the help of their daughter, Nia, provide all their customers with a warm and friendly welcome that is part and parcel of the superb hospitality of the inn. Open each day at 16.00 and all day from Friday to Sunday, this well recommended pub is known throughout the area for its excellent range of real ales, beers, and lagers that are served from the bar. The traditional, cosy interior, with a roaring fire in winter, is the perfect place to come to for a relaxing drink and a chat with friends. To further add to the enjoyment of an evening at The Star, the family also organise the occasional quiz night and kareoke evening.

RHEWL   MAP 4 REF I4
5 miles SE of Denbigh on the A525

Found in **Rhewl**, just to the north of Ruthin, is **The Drovers Arms**, an attractive black and white pub that is rather special as they brew their own beer. Owners, Sharon and Charles Gale-Hasleham, ensure that their beers, Doctor Johnson, Drovers Special, St David's Celebration, Jolly Jack Tar (a porter beer), Shepherd's Celebration, and Four Thumbs reach the bar in tip top condition and are on tap at all times. It is certainly worth travelling here to taste these beers but also to sample the other delights of this charming pub. Closed on Monday lunchtimes, but open all day at the weekend, The Drovers Arms not only promises an excellent pint of ale but is also well regarded for the delicious pub meals that are served through-

The Drovers Arms, Rhewl, near Ruthin, Denbighshire LL15 1UD
Tel: 01824 703163

out. Cosy and full of character inside, with a number of intimate snug areas, there is also a pleasant beer garden complete with children's toys, a slide, and a safe climbing tree.

PWLL-GLÂS   MAP 4 REF I4
7 miles SE of Denbigh on the A494

Just south of Ruthin, at Pwll-glâs, lies the **Fox and Hounds Inn**, a charming pub that has been owned and personally run by Stephen Bethell since 1965, and more recently with the help of his daughter, Emma. A popular and well recommended inn locally, this attractive white building is hard

Fox and Hounds Inn, Pwll-glâs, Denbighshire LL15 2PG
Tel: 01824 703137

to miss and certainly worth while taking a detour to find. Well known for its superb selection of real ales, plus lagers, stouts, and ciders, the enviable reputation of the Fox and Hounds is built upon the excellent menu that is served at both lunchtime (except Mondays) and in the evening. Although no bookings are needed at this stylish and comfortable pub, those arriving late may find the inn full, particularly on Thursday evening, which is fish night. Purchased fresh from the market that morning the beautifully prepared dishes complement the usual menu that includes such delicious favourite as steaks and mixed grills. To further add to the attraction of the Fox and Hounds, Stephen and Emma have recently opened an extension to the inn that incorporates 14 excellent en-suite guest bedrooms.

LLANARMON-YN IAL
MAP 4 REF J4
10 miles SE of Denbigh on B5431

Found in an attractive position on the banks of the River Alun, at the southern end of the Clwydian Range, this small village has an interesting church with two naves.

Tucked away in Llanarmon-yn Ial, **The Raven Inn** is a hidden gem that is well worth seeking out. Very popular locally and highly recommended for its fine ales and delicious food, it is perhaps the pleasant and relaxing atmosphere that tenants, Jan and Chris Fussell have created that makes this inn so special. Dating back to 1722 and then known as The Village Inn, the pub used to brew its own beer. It was the village postman who, having shot one of the biggest ravens any of the villagers had ever seen, instigated the pub's name change by presenting the dead bird to the then publican. The raven, now stuffed and mounted, still stands on display in the bar.

The Raven Inn, Ffordd Rhiw Ial, Llanarmon-yn Ial
Denbighshire CH7 4QE Tel & Fax: 01824 780787/780307

Open all day, every day (except Monday and Tuesday lunchtimes in January and February), the Raven not only serves a wide range of real ales from the bar but there is also a bar menu as well as a cosy restaurant, for which bookings are generally needed. Whether it is a light snack or a hearty meal, the menus are sure to satisfy everyone and the charming interior decor makes the whole experience exceedingly pleasant.

LLANFAIR DYFFRYN CLWYD   MAP 4 REF I4
8 miles S of Denbigh on A525

The 15th-century church, in this small village, has a 17th-century Communion table and a mosaic window of 15th-century glass.

LLANFIHANGEL GLYN MYFYR   MAP 4 REF H4
11 miles S of Denbigh on B5105

This sleepy village lies in the fertile vale through which the River Alwen runs and, just to the north lies the **Clocaenog Forest**, Wales' second largest commercial plantation which covers much of the southern moorland between the vales of Clwyd and Conwy. Managed by the Forestry Commission, there is a gamekeeper's cottage off the B5105 that has been converted into a Visitor Centre. From here there are well marked Forest Trails, varying in length, that lead walkers through the mixed plantation of larch, spruce, pine, beech, oak, and ash.

Llyn Brenig, on the edge of the forest, is a massive, man-made reservoir that was completed in 1976 to accompany the smaller Llyn Alwen which was constructed in the early 1900s. Close to the dam is a Visitors Centre which explains the local history and ecology as well as acting as a starting point for lakeside walks. By the lake, depending on the time of year, butterflies such as the Orange Tip and the Tortoiseshell can be seen. The lake can also be fished and there are opportunities for sailing, canoeing, and windsurfing.

Set amidst the glorious countryside of Mynydd Hiraethog and just north of Llyn Brenig, **The Sportsmans Arms** is the highest inn in Wales. Found by the side of an old turnpike road that was constructed in 1824 by the famous builder John Sinclair, the inn dates from 1829. Today this very Welsh pub, where the language is still spoken on a daily basis, is managed by Bethan and Bob Hughes, a charming couple who maintain the tradition of offering travellers the very best in hospitality. Well decorated and furnished throughout, this olde worlde pub has, at its heart, a wood burning stove to ensure that all receive a warm welcome whatever the weather outside. Open all day during the summer and for the evening in the winter months, The Sportsmans Arms not only offers its customers a fine selection of Lee's ales but also delicious home-cooked bar snacks and meals

**The Sportsmans Arms, Bryntrillyn, Bylchau, near Denbigh
Denbighshire LL16 5SW Tel: 01745 550214**

are available. For the enjoyment of locals and visitors alike, Bethan and Bob also provide entertainment, in the form of Welsh singing, on Saturday evenings - a treat not to be missed.

CERRIGYDRUDION
MAP 4 REF H5

13 miles S of Denbigh on A5

This village's name, often misspelt as 'druidion', means Place of the Brave and as such has no connections with Druids. There are many tales of fairy cattle to be found in Wales and they are thought to have been descended from the aurochs, the wild cattle that roamed Britain in prehistoric times. Cerrigydrudion has its own cow, Y Fuwch Frech (the freckled cow), who lived on nearby Hiraethog mountain. For years she supplied the area with milk and would always fill any receptacle brought to her. One day, a witch began to milk her into a sieve and continued until the cow went insane and drowned herself in Llyn Dau Ychen.

The impressive **Saracen's Head Travel Inn** dates back to the late 16th century and it stands on land once owned by the Knights Templar with the site of a notorious 8th-century battle, in which 1000 men are believed to have lost their lives, nearby. Now an excellent and highly regarded hotel, inn, and eating place, the Saracen's Head successfully combines its traditional character and charm with superb up-to-date facilities.

The cosy restaurant seats 50 people in comfort and is open all day for delicious morning coffees, lunches, afternoon teas, and evening meals. The à la carte menu offers a mouth-watering range of steaks, fish, meat, and games dishes, as well as an appetising selection of starters and desserts, and the owners, Sue and Nigel Moxon share the creation of these dishes. Advance booking is advisable on Friday and Saturday evenings

**The Saracen's Head Travel Inn, Cerrigydrudion
Denbighshire LL21 9SY Tel: 01490 420327 Fax: 01490 420405**

and for Sunday lunch. Though food is important, this is not all the Saracen's Head Travel Inn has to offer as not only is there a well stocked bar but also six charming en-suite guest rooms.

6 Gateway to Wales

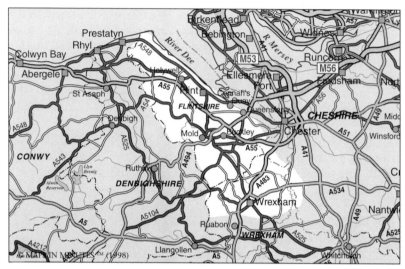

The gateway to Wales, often missed by many visitors to the country as they speed westwards, has a rich history that lies beneath its often industrial past. The Romans certainly forayed into the area from their major town of Chester and there is also evidence of Celtic settlements here. However, it was during the 13th century that Edward I, after his successful campaign against the Welsh, set about building his ambitious Iron Ring of huge fortresses along the north Wales coast. Each of the castles was built one day's march from the next and the first stronghold of this fearsome ring was begun at Flint in 1277. Now all but ruins, this massive project, the largest seen in Europe, was able to contain Edward's adversary, Llewelyn the Last, to the west of the country.

As well as being a strategic area, keenly fought over for centuries, the land around the Dee estuary is, more peacefully, the home to great numbers of waders and wildfowl who feed on the mudflats left by the retreating tides. Between the estuary and the Clwydian Range lie small, compact villages as well as the market town of Mold and Holywell, a place of pilgrimages that became known as the Lourdes of Wales.

Further south lies Wrexham, another ancient market place that has a connection with Yale University in America, and the charming border town of Bangor-is-y-coed, with its attractive and informal National Hunt race course. Though this gateway to the country is a relatively small region, it can however boast several of the Seven Wonders of Wales: the Bells of Gresford's church; St Winefride's Well, Holywell; the Overton Yew Trees; and the steeple of St Giles' Church, Wrexham.

MOLD

The small county town of Flintshire, Mold, like many other towns in the area who boast famous sons, is proud to claim the novelist Daniel Owen as one of its own. Known as the Welsh Dickens, his statue stands outside the library where there is a memorial room exhibiting items from his lifetime. For visitors who are interested in history, **St Mary's Church**, dating from the 15th century, has some interesting stained glass windows and architectural ornamentation whilst, at **Bailey Hill**, the remains of a Norman motte and bailey can be seen.

On the outskirts of town, **Theatr Clwyd** offers a wide range of entertainment for the culturally hungry with its lively and widely acclaimed theatre and frequent exhibitions of art, sculpture, and photography.

The composer Felix Mendelssohn was said to have been inspired by the town's surroundings when writing his opus *Rivulet*. The limestone crags provide panoramic views over the surrounding country and there are lovely spots for picnics to be found.

Just to the west of Mold can be found **Loggerheads Country Park**, situated on the edge of the Clwydian Range and a formally recognised Area of Outstanding Natural Beauty of some 62 square miles. This is a wonderful environment for all the family, especially the young ones, to wander around and enjoy following various trails which are each about one and a half miles long. They all start near the mill building and separate trail guides are available giving detailed information for: The Industrial Trail, Nature Trail, and Squirrel Nuttley Children's Trail. The mill, built in about 1790, used water from the river to drive a water wheel and two sets of stones to grind corn from the local farms. It is now fully restored and can be seen at close quarters.

Some 200 years ago, Loggerheads was part of the leadmining industry founded on ore-bearing limestone, and many relics remain and can be seen within the quiet woodland. There is a fine selection of local arts and crafts and souvenirs on display in the Craft Shop at the **Loggerheads Countryside Centre**, and the tea rooms and gardens are always popular. This is a great day out with lots to explore whatever the season and at a very low cost.

The smooth browned slopes of the Clwydian Range ascend from the broad and fertile planes of the Vale of Clwyd to the west and **Moel Famau** (the Mother of Mountains), at 1,820 feet, is the highest peak. It is well worth the climb, not only to discover the remains of a **Jubilee Tower** built in 1810 to commemorate King George III's Golden Jubilee (blown down in a storm in 1852) but also to take in the breathtaking, panoramic views: westwards to the Vale of Clwyd with its river stretching down to the Irish Sea and to the east where the land rolls gently down to the Dee estuary.

Found in the heart of the town, **The Leeswood Arms** is one of Mold's oldest buildings, dating back over 250 years, and, at one time, it was home

to the town's court room. Today, however, nobody stands in judgement as landlord and lady, Barry and Joyce Probert serve their customers a range of real ales, beers, and lagers. Open all day, every day, though no food is available here, Barry and Joyce are happy for customers to bring their own and enjoy a pint or two with their lunch. The delightful interior reflects the age of the building and the low beamed ceilings make the two drinking areas very cosy and atmospheric. Each is individually themed, one on horse racing and the

The Leeswood Arms, Wrexham Street, Mold
Flintshire CH7 1HQ Tel: 01352 753950

other with motor racing memorabilia and, with the addition of the occasional entertainment at Bank Holidays, this is a popular town centre pub.

NORTH OF MOLD

RHYDYMWYN   MAP 4 REF J3
2 miles NW of Mold on the A451

At Rhydymwyn, just a couple of miles northwest of Mold, lies **The Antelope**, a charming family run inn that dates back over 200 years. Although Heather and Gwynne Williams, who purchased the inn in July 1998, have only been here a short time, they have certainly made their mark. As well as giving the pub its old name back, they have also undertaken a refurbishment programme which has highlighted the old features of the characterful inn. The pleasant and cosy restaurant area is ideal for all the

The Antelope, Rhydymwyn, near Mold, Flintshire CH7 5HE
Tel: 01352 741247

family, and a comprehensive and varied menu of delicious meals is served here throughout the day. Going hand in hand with the superb food is the excellent selection of well-kept real ales. With plenty of outdoor seating for fine weather, and the warm and friendly interior for cooler days and the winter, this is a lovely pub that is sure to go from strength to strength.

PANTASAPH   MAP 4 REF I3
9 miles NW of Mold off A55

The Franciscan Friary, surrounding the 19th-century village church, is visited by many people throughout the year who come to take advantage of the peaceful surroundings and gardens.

WHITFORD   MAP 4 REF I3
10 miles NW of Mold off A5151

Close to the village can be found a curious monument, **Maen Achwyfaen** (the Stone of Lamentation). This Celtic cross, sculptured in a wheel shape, is said to have been erected in about 1000 to commemorate a person or event unknown and it is the tallest such cross in Britain. The renowned 18th-century travel writer, Thomas Pennant, is buried in the graveyard adjacent to the grand 19th-century church.

TRELAWNYD
MAP 4 REF I3

13 miles NW of Mold on A5151

Gop Hill, with its Bronze Age cairn, is the spot where, traditionally, Offa's Dyke begins, or ends, though Prestatyn, to the north, also holds this honour. The dyke stretches along the Welsh border down to Chepstow and was built by King Offa of Mercia while in the process of defining and fortifying his powerful kingdom. Today, a footpath, opened in 1971, follows the route but solitary expeditions are inadvisable, especially during bad weather.

LLANASA
MAP 4 REF I2

13 miles NW of Mold off A5151

Close by the village, **Gyrn Castle** (open to the public), originates from the 1700s and was castellated in the 1820. It contains a large picture gallery and pleasant woodland walks can be taken in its grounds.

POINT OF AYR
MAP 4 REF I2

14 miles NW of Mold off A548

Marking the western tip of the Dee estuary, this designated RSPB viewing point is an excellent place to see the numerous birds that come to feed on the sands and mudflats left by the retreating tide.

HOLYWELL
MAP 4 REF J3

8 miles N of Mold on A5026

Referred to as one of the Seven Wonders of Wales, **St Winefride's Well**, in the town, was once a place of pilgrimage likened to Lourdes in France. According to tradition, Winefride, the daughter of Prince Tewyth, was beheaded by Prince Cradoc after refusing his advances. It is claimed that a spring gushed from the place where her head fell and that she returned to life. Winefride (Gwenfrewi in Welsh) went on to become an abbess at Gwytherin Convent near Llanrwst. Thought to have healing qualities, the well, has been visited by pilgrims since the 7th century and still is, particularly on St Winefride's Day, the nearest Saturday to 22 June.

St Winefride's Well, Holywell

St Winefride's Chapel sits on top of the Greenfield Valley Heritage Park, an area of lakeside and woodland walks, built on the site where textiles, copper, and brass were once produced. Built around 1500 to enclose three sides of the well, the chapel was paid for by Henry VII's mother, Margaret Beaufort. The park is also home to the Abbey Farm Agriculture Museum on a working farm. The trail through the park leads down towards the coast and to the ruins of Basingwerk Abbey. Built by Cistercian monks in 1132, it functioned as a self-sufficient abbey; Cistercians laying great emphasis upon agricultural labour. Although an English foundation, Basingwerk absorbed Welsh culture and the Welsh bard, Gutun Owain, was associated with the Abbey from where he wrote *The Chronicle of Princes* also known as the *Black Book of Basingwerk*.

Basingwerk Abbey, near Holywell

The abbey survived until the Dissolution of Monasteries in the 16th century by Henry VIII. In a tranquil setting which contrasts with the busy roads not far away, this magnificent ruin contains a Norman arch that, despite weather beaten columns and faded 'messages of love', is a fine example of that architecture. In one of the buildings the remains of timber beams can be seen which once supported a roof.

Holywell is also home to an unusual underground military museum, the Grange Cavern Museum, which contains a whole host of military vehicles in a cave scooped out of the hillside.

**The White Lion Inn, Glan yr Afon, Holywell, Flintshire CH8 9BQ
Tel: 01745 560280**

Lying in the tucked away village of **Glan yr Afon**, near Holywell, is
The White Lion Inn, a delightful Grade II listed building that dates back
to the early 1700s. The former home of the famous Welsh playwright,
Emlyn Williams, this olde worlde pub has been owned and personally run
by Val and Chris Mellor since 1987. Surrounded by beautiful, well tended
gardens that are not only home to a wealth of wildlife but also some strut-
ting peacocks, the pub and its setting are idyllic.

Open every evening and also at lunchtimes at the weekend, this is the
place to come to for excellent real ale and delicious food. As well as the
usual John Smith's, Webster's, and Yorkshire beers, there is a different guest
ale each week served at the bar. Well renowned for its menu, the tasty
array of tempting dishes could certainly not be classed as pub grub and a
meal here is one to be relished. With a warm and friendly atmosphere,
and the added attraction of a pianist each Friday evening, The White Lion
Inn is well worth finding for those who look for fine food and drink in
pleasant company.

MOSTYN   MAP 4 REF I2
11 miles N of Mold on the A548

Just outside Mostyn, in the village of **Llanerch-y-Mor** to the north of

**Ye Olde Tavern Inn, Llanerch-y-Mor, near Mostyn
Flintshire CH8 9DX Tel: 01745 560482**

Holywell, lies **Ye Olde Tavern Inn**, which must be one of the most unusual premises in the country. Originally two buildings, half of the inn is an old chapel dating back to the 11th century whilst the other half is a 16th-century former farmhouse turned alehouse. As the chapel is of special architectural note, the charm and character of this ancient building is safeguarded from overzealous reconstruction work and, today, it is home to the restaurant area of the pub. Peter Jones, the landlord, and his manager, Belinda Thomas, take great delight in serving a range of delicious home-cooked meals in this cosy area which, as might be imagined, is full of character and olde worlde charm. The main bar area, and a larger restaurant area, can be found in the 'newer' farmhouse part of the inn. Open all day, and every day from Easter to the end of October, not only is the bar well stocked with a wide range of drinks and at least three real ales but customers can enjoy the same menu of tasty dishes at the monthly Saturday evening dinner dances. Booking for these popular events is essential and customers should look out for the forthcoming medieval banquets held in the chapel.

FLINT   MAP 4 REF J3
6 miles N of Mold on A548

This small and modest town can boast two interesting historical facts. Firstly, it was the site of the first of Edward I's Iron Ring fortresses and, secondly, the associated borough was the first in Wales to receive a charter (in 1284). Dotted along the North Wales coast, a day's march apart, Edward I's Iron Ring of massive fortresses represented Europe's most ambitious and concentrated medieval building project. Started after the Treaty of Aberconwy in 1277 and completed in 1284, **Flint Castle**, now in ruins, overlooks the coastal marshes of the Dee Estuary. Originally surrounded by a water-filled moat, the remains of the Great Tower or Donjon are an impressive sight. Flint Castle featured in the downfall of Richard II, when he was lured here in 1399 from the relative safety of Conwy Castle and captured by Henry Bolingbroke, the Duke of Lancaster and future King Henry IV. In Shakespeare's play *Richard II*, in response to Bolingbroke's, "My gracious Lord, I come but for mine own", the defeated King replies, "Your own is yours, and I am yours, and all". At this point even the King's faithful greyhound is said to have deserted him.

During the Civil War, Flint remained Royalist until it was taken, in 1647, by General Mytton, who was responsible for dismantling the castle into the ruins seen today.

HALKYN
MAP 4 REF J3
5 miles N of Mold off A55

The village lies close to Halkyn Mountain, the ridge of which rises to 964 feet and is scarred by the remnants of ancient lead mines.

Dating back to the 18th century, **The Bluebell Inn** occupies a superb position up in the Halkyn hills and it is real a country pub as there are tie ups for horses, with a drinking trough, outside. Owned since January 1998 by John Fisher and ably managed by Emma and Alan Vaughan, this charming inn is ideal for those looking for a quiet drink and a tasty meal at any time of day. As befits a building of this age, the interior is full of character, with exposed ceiling beams, leaded windows, and a delightful Victorian fireplace and, outside, there is a flagged beer garden that proves

The Bluebell Inn, Rhosesmor Road, Halkyn, Flintshire CH8 8DL
Tel: 01352 780309

to be a real sun trap. As well as serving a well chosen range of ales, beers, and lagers at the bar, The Bluebell Inn offers its customers an extensive menu of bar snacks and meals that are sure to suit all the family. Entertainment, in various forms, is provided with a quiz night each Wednesday, traditional Welsh singing on Friday evenings, and live music on Saturday nights. Those who enjoy the delights of The Bluebell Inn will be interested to learn that John also owns and runs The Swan Inn at St Asaph.

RHOSESMOR   MAP 4 REF J3
2 miles N of Mold on B5123

Moel y Gaer, near this small village, was considered to be a fine example of a Iron Age hillfort until archeological digs unearthed evidence that suggested habitation from as far back as 3500 BC.

Found in the quiet village of **Northop Hall**, just to the east of Rhosesmor, **The Black Lion**, is locally known by the interesting name of the Bottom Monkey. Whilst the reason for the pub's unusual nickname is unknown it is thought to come from either the name given to the tool into which gunpowder was placed before blasting in the nearby, now disused, pits or after the man who operated it. Open every day, except non-Bank Holiday Monday lunchtimes, this attractive pub is run by Susan and Keith Gordon Jones, both former practising lawyers, who it could be said have gone from bar to bar. The interior, with its exposed wall and ceiling beams and brick and stone fireplace, is decorated with all manner of ornaments and memorabilia; there is a water jug and beer stein collection hanging from the ceiling beams and the fireplace is decorated with a mass of brass objects.

The Black Lion, Village Road, Northop Hall, Flintshire CH7 6HT
Tel: 01244 815982

This is a popular pub, well known for its fine selection of well kept ales, that also has a good local reputation for the menu of home-made meals and snacks which are served both in the restaurant and in the bar area. Supplemented by a list of daily specials, as well as the classic pub dishes, there are some interesting and more exotic meals that are sure to tempt all who feel peckish. Meals are served daily and anyone wishing to eat here at the weekend should book first to avoid disappointment.

Set within its own private grounds and approached by a fine avenue of lime trees, **Soughton Hall**, just to the south of Northop, is a splendid house that was built in 1714 as a Bishop's Palace. The home of the Rodenhurst family today, this delightful house has been the property of the Wynne-Bankes family for many years and much of the building as it now appears was due to the work of William John Bankes in the 1820s. Following extensive restoration work, Rosemary and John Rodenhurst, with the help of their son, Simon, have opened the hall as a relaxing and informal family hotel that is also one of the country's more magnificent stately homes.

The historical stables, within the hotel's grounds, have also been restored and here can be found **The Stables** restaurant and bar, a superb place for a quiet meal in unusual and interesting surroundings. With many of the original building's features remaining, dinners can enjoy a drink at the bar created from the old stable stalls, before moving through to the delightful restaurant area that was the original hay loft. Simon, an accom-

The Stables at Soughton Hall, Northop, near Chester
Flintshire CH7 6AB Tel: 01352 840577 Fax: 01352 840382

plished chef, oversees the kitchens where the extensive and varied menu of interesting dishes are freshly prepared to order in full view of the restaurant. The unusual style of The Stables, along with this superb location and surroundings, is perfect for an evening out that compliments beautifully the more formal dining arrangements at the hall.

EWLOE
MAP 4 REF J3
4 miles NE of Mold on A550

Hidden in a steeply wooded glen lie the ruins of **Ewloe Castle**. Originally an English stronghold which fell into the hands of the Welsh in about 1146, it was being fortified by Owain Gwynedd as an ambush castle when the Battle of Eulo took place in 1157. In the early 13th century an apsidal Welsh tower, two wards protected by a curtain wall, and an outer ditch were added but the castle was never of any great importance. After the completion of Flint Castle in the late 13th century Ewloe Castle ceased to have any military significance at all.

HAWARDEN
MAP 4 REF J3
5 miles W of Mold off A550

Mentioned in the Doomsday Book, this village boasts two castles: one a ruin dating from the 13th century and, another, that was once the home of the Victorian Prime Minister, William Gladstone. **Harwarden Castle**, Gladstone's home for some 60 years, was started in 1750 and enlarged and castellated by Sir Stephen Glynne in 1809. The remains, chiefly the circular keep and the hall, of the older castle stand in **Castle Park**.

The Parish Church, as well as having stained glass by Burne-Jones, also houses the **Gladstone Memorial Chapel**, where the marble effigies of the distinguished statesman and his wife, both of whom are buried in Westminster Abbey, can be seen. The village's connections with Gladstone continue to this day as the statesman donated his collection of books to the famous **St Deinol's Residential Library** which lies adjacent to the church.

SOUTH OF MOLD

CAERGWRLE
MAP 4 REF J4
5 miles SE of Mold off A541

Once a Roman station occupied by legions from Chester, the fortification probably started life as a Bronze Age hillfort. Built more or less in its present form by Dafydd, brother of Llewelyn the Last, it was from this border fort, in 1282, that Dafydd launched the last, and fatal, Welsh rebellion against Edward I.

The Bridge Inn, Pontblyddyn, near Mold, Flintshire CH7 4HN
Tel: 01352 770087

Just to the north, at **Pontblyddyn**, can be found **The Bridge Inn**, a charming pub dating back to the late 16th century which combines the very best in beer and food in stylish and elegant surroundings. Managed by Chris and Wendi, the pub has a real olde worlde atmosphere and it is likely that, should Captain Henry Morgan walk in here today he would find himself in familiar surroundings. Perhaps the inn's most famous visitor, this was where Henry Morgan courted a local girl, Jenny Jones, before he left for the Caribbean and his attacks against the Spanish which eventually lead to his becoming the Lieutenant Governor of Jamaica in the late 17th century.

Though the olde worlde setting may not have changed, the high quality of the delicious food and drink served here most surely has. Well known locally for its extensive menu of bar snacks and restaurant meals, The Bridge Inn is certainly the place for a celebration meal out where quality dishes are combined with a excellent service in the wonderful restaurant. The main bar, with its original 400-year-old exposed beams and magnificent stone fireplace, is very much the haunt of those looking for a delicious pint of real ale. The gardens too are as pretty as a picture and with entertainment on Monday evenings, The Bridge Inn is well worth a visit but customers should remember to book if they wish to eat here at the weekends.

BWLCH GWYN
7 miles S of Mold on A525

MAP 4 REF J4

On the border with Flintshire, the village is home to the **Geological and Folk Museum of North Wales**. The museum holds information on the geology of the area and how man adapted to the challenges of this environment.

**The Westminster Arms, Ruthin Road, Bwlch Gwyn
Wrexham LL11 5UT Tel: 01978 753875**

The Westminster Arms, in the heart of the village, has been owned and personally run by the young, but experienced, couple, Kerry and Tim Shaw, since the beginning of 1998. In that time they have not only extended the premises by creating an attractive and comfortable eating lounge, but also established the pub's reputation in the area as a place where fine food, good ale, and pleasant company is very much order of the day. With an excellent selection of beers and ales on tap at the bar, the delicious menu of traditional pub dishes, created by Tim, the chef of the partnership, makes this an ideal pub to come to with all the family. Open every day, and all day Saturday and Sunday during the football season, The Westminster Arms also provides its customers with occasional evening entertainment and there are enthusiastic darts, pool, and football teams based here.

WREXHAM   MAP 4 REF J4
10 miles S of Mold on A451

This once small market town is now a busy place that has plenty to offer the visitor. There are a variety of markets still held here today, in **Eagles Meadow**, the largest being on Mondays. However, a more interesting experience for city dwellers might be the cattle market held on Saturdays where farmers from surrounding area come to socialise and oversee business transactions and where visitors can wander around soaking in this rural atmosphere.

For those wanting to find out more about the town then the **Heritage Centre** in King Street is worth the visit. Wrexham's history has been traced back to the Bronze Age, after 'Brymbo Man', was uncovered by workmen. The Romans were also in the area and developed many industries over the centuries. People too have played their part in the town's history and Acton, a suburb of Wrexham, was the birthplace of Judge Jeffreys, nicknamed 'Bloody' for his apparent lack of compassion and belief in swift justice.

Perhaps the town's best known building, particularly to American tourists, is the **Church of St Giles** which dominates the town's skyline and where Elihu Yale, the benefactor of Yale University, was buried after his death in 1721. Yale's tomb was restored in 1968 by members of Yale University to mark the 250th anniversary of the benefaction and it can be found in the churchyard to the west of the tower. The church is itself of great interest and is recognised as one of the Seven Wonders of Wales. Begun in 1506, though much restored, the tower still carries some of the original medieval carvings and, in particular, those of St Giles which are recognisable by his attributes of an arrow and a deer.

Just to the south of the town lies **Erddig Country Park**, a National Trust property of some 2000 acres. Within the park is also the late 17th-century mansion that is equipped as it was during its heyday. Begun by a Joshua Edisbury, the High Sheriff of Denbighshire, who fled unable to meet his debts, the mansion was held by the Meller family and their de-

Erddig, Wrexham

scendants until it was given to the National Trust in 1973. The mansion contains many fine examples of period pieces of furniture and an interesting collection of portraits of the staff. The country park has fine gardens which have been restored to their 18th-century plan.

Along with Erddig and Bersham Ironworks, also lying within the **Clywedog Valley and Trail** is **King's Mill**, a restored mill that dates from 1769 although an older mill has been on the site since 1315. The principal feature here is 'The Miller's Tale', a presentation which depicts the life and work of a miller in 1769.

Just a stone's throw from Wrexham's main street lies **Brady's Bar**, a superb Irish pub, as its name suggests, that is owned by Julie Bell. This early 18th-century, listed building is hard to miss and its original name, The Swan, can still be seen above the door. In fact, for many years, The Swan was not only a pub but it also brewed its own beer. Though those days have long gone, stepping into Brady's Bar is certainly like taking a step back in time. Very cosy and comfortable inside, with wooden floors and half-panelled walls, there is all manner of memorabilia, including many old prints of Dublin, and background Irish music to help create the Gaelic atmosphere. Naturally, many of the beers and real ales served at the bar are from Ireland and, as well as the familiar brews, there are some less well known. For fine, sunny days, customers can also take advantage of the outdoor patio area which is also an excellent suntrap.

Brady's Bar, 6 Abbot Street, Wrexham, LL11 1TA
Tel: 01978 313039

GRESFORD   Map 4 ref K4
9 miles SE of Mold on B5445

This former coal mining town was the site of a mine explosion in 1934 which killed 266 men. The colliery closed in 1973 but the wheel remains in memory of those killed in the disaster. All Saints' Church is one of the finest in Wales and it also houses the famous **Gresford Bells**, another of the Seven Wonders of Wales, that are played on Tuesdays and Sundays.

Found hidden away on Gresford's former main street, **The Yew Tree Inn** lies adjacent to the parish church. Dating back to the 1700s, this former coaching inn was originally built as three cottages and was, at one time, the village armoury. Today, however, its role in village life, as the central meeting place for both locals and visitors, has been very well established by the landlord David Walker with the help of his wife Jacqui.

**The Yew Tree Inn, Church Green, High Street, Gresford
Wrexham LL12 8RF Tel: 01978 852566**

Completely redecorated inside in the summer of 1998, The Yew Tree Inn is open all day from Friday to Sunday, and Bank Holidays, and every day throughout the week. The emphasis here is very much on good quality beer and there is a fine range of real ales, beers, and lagers behind the bar and, occasionally, sandwiches and pies are available to those who feel peckish. A lively and friendly pub, there is a singer every Friday evening, alternate Saturday nights feature live music, and, once a week, everyone's general knowledge is tested in the enjoyable pub quiz.

HOLT   Map 4 ref K4
13 miles SE of Mold on A534

The River Dee, which marks the border with England, runs through this village and its importance as a crossing place can be seen in the 15th-century bridge. The village was also the site of a Roman pottery works that provided material for the fort at Chester.

BANGOR-IS-Y-COED   Map 4 ref K5
15 miles SE of Mold on A525

Also known as **Bangor-on-Dee**, the village is well known to racegoers for its picturesque course which holds meetings throughout the National Hunt season. The village itself has a charming 17th-century bridge which is said to have been built by Inigo Jones. There are also claims that the Romans might have been here but the likelihood is that they were in Holt as the pottery works there are firmer evidence of their presence in the area.

Bangor was, however, the site of a Celtic monastery founded around AD 180, which was destroyed in 607 by Ethelfrid of Northumbria in the what was the last victory by Saxons over Celtic Christianity. Apparently, 1200 monks were laid to sword as Ethelfrid considered praying against him was tantamount to fighting against him. Those fortunate enough to have survived are thought to have gone to Bardsey Island. Legend has it that Owain Glyndwr married Margaret Hamner in the hamlet of Hammer four miles away.

When Kathleen and David White bought **The Stableyard**, Bangor-is-y-coed's oldest building, over 25 years ago, it was lying derelict after having

**The Stableyard, High Street, Bangor-is-y-coed, Wrexham LL13 0AU
Tel: 01978 780642 Fax: 01978781167**

been a coaching inn since the 1630s, a butcher's shop in the 1920s, and finally, a coffee bar. Now lovingly restored and refurbished in a manner reflecting the age of the property, this delightful restaurant is fast gaining a reputation as one of the best in north Wales. Offering a true taste of European country cooking, David, the chef of the partnership with the help of apprentice Daniel, create a menu of classic dishes that utilise a wealth of fresh ingredients. Open every day during the morning and each evening, except Sunday and Monday evenings, The Stableyard is an excellent place to come to for morning coffee or a special celebration meal out. Those lucky enough to be visiting the area can also take advantage of The Stableyard's six comfortable guest rooms that, like the rest of the establishment, have a charming olde worlde atmosphere with furnishings to match.

OVERTON   MAP 4 REF K5
16 miles S of Mold on A539

This substantial border village is home to another of the Seven Wonders of Wales. In this case 21 yew trees, the **Overton Yew Trees**, that stand in the churchyard of the village Church of St Mary. Dating from medieval times, the trees have a preservation order on them. Within the church itself are some interesting artefacts from the 13th century.

7 Llangollen and the Ruabon Mountains

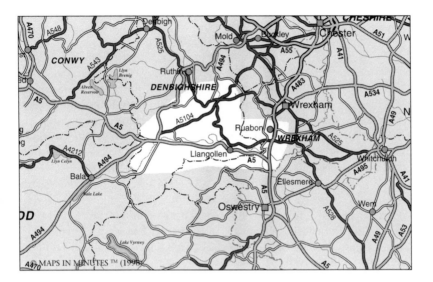

This area of Wales, centred around the valley of the River Dee, the Vale of Llangollen, is certainly one of variety. Llangollen, a delightful old town in a picturesque riverside setting below Ruabon Mountain, is not only a charming place to visit with some surprising attractions, but also home to the annual International Music Eisteddfod. An eisteddfod was, originally, a meeting of bards where prizes were awarded for poetry reading and singing. Though small village events and the annual Royal National Eisteddfod still draw people from all over the country and beyond, the event at Llangollen has a true international flavour and Luciano Pavarotti has graced its stage.

Further north lies, by way of a contrast, the Clywedog Valley that was once a hot bed of industrialisation during the 18th century. Using the power of the River Clywedog, factories and mills sprang up in the valley whose chief product was iron. As the Industrial Revolution progressed and other forms of power became available, the factories moved away from the valley but the remains are here for all to discover. The industrial trail along the Clywedog Valley takes in the Minera Lead Mines, Nant Mill, and Bersham Ironworks as well as a section of Offa's Dyke and a wealth of plant and bird life.

Thomas Telford, once dubbed the 'Colossus of Roads', was also active in the area and just to the east of Llangollen can be found Pontcysyllte Aqueduct, a great feat of engineering upon which much of Telford's reputation was built. North Wales is also home to another Telford construction, the still much used London to Holyhead Turnpike (the A5) which runs through Snowdonia. But, perhaps, the pioneering engineer's greatest achievement was the Menai Suspension Bridge, which still links the mainland with the Isle of Anglesey.

LLANGOLLEN

This busy yet picturesque town draws visitors from all over the world, particularly to the annual **International Music Eisteddfod** during July which, since first being held here in 1947, now attracts something like 12,000 participants. For six days the town is awash with colour, costume, and a wide variety of musical genres. However, there are many other attractions to keep visitors satisfied during the rest of the year.

The town's name is derived from St Collen who founded the parish church here between the late 6th and early 7th century. The church, which is still standing, has been much restored and refurbished over the years. A local story tells of how St Collen, after fighting with a giantess in a nearby pass, washed off the blood in a well, known locally as Ffynnon Collen (St Collen's Well).

Plas Newydd, situated off Queen Street, is an attractive half-timbered house that was the home of the 'Ladies of Llangollen' - Lady Eleanor Butler and Sarah Ponsonby. Eccentric Irishwomen, the two ladies left their homes to eventually settle in Llangollen where they altered the small cottage into the house seen today. Devoting their lives to 'friendship, celibacy, and the knitting of blue stockings', they became celebrities who attracted many famous visitors to the town: Walter Scott, William Wordsworth, and the Duke of Wellington to mention but a few. With a passion for collecting curios, their displays was added to by their many visitors but much of the collection was dispersed after their deaths. Yet, even so, a visit is worthwhile particularly to see the oak panelling and stained glass windows inside the house and the surrounding gardens.

Back in the town centre and spanning the River Dee is an eye-catching bridge dating from 1347 when it was first constructed by John Trevor, who went on to become the Bishop of St Asaph. The four-arched bridge has since been rebuilt and widened in places to accommodate the changing demands of traffic through the times.

On the northside of the river is **Llangollen Station**, home of the Llangollen Railway Society. Since taking over the disused line in 1975, the society has restored the railway track and journeys along the River Dee can be taken on this delightful narrow gauge steam railway. At the moment the route goes as far as Carrog but the aim is to restore the line as far as Corwen. The station houses a museum with a collection of engines, coaches, and other rail memorabilia.

On the banks of the Llangollen branch of the Shropshire Union Canal is the **Canal Museum** and just a short walk from the Wharf is **Castell Dinas Bran**. Although the remains of this Iron Age hillfort are not substantial the views from the top are worth the effort. A more modern attraction is the world's largest permanent **Doctor Who Exhibition**. Though Llangollen may seem an unusual place for the collection of artefacts and memorabilia associated with the time traveller, Doctor Who fans, young and old, will enjoy a visit.

Taking the road north out of Llangollen the route passes the impressive ruins of **Valle Crucis Abbey**. This Cistercian abbey was founded in 1201 by Madog ap Gruffyd, the Prince of Powys, and was ideally situated for the austere monks as this was a remote spot beneath the steep-sided mountains. Despite a fire, the tower collapsing, and then the Dissolution in 1535, the ruins are in good condition and visitors can obtain a 'feel' for how the monks once lived. Among the original masonry, magnificent pillars and windows still to be seen, are some mutilated tombs, thought to include that of Iolo Goch, a bard of Owain Glyndwr, and domestic buildings.

Valle Crucis, near Llangollen

About half a mile from the abbey stands **Eliseg's Pillar** erected in the early 9th century and, in fact, valle crucis means valley of the cross. The inscription on this Christian memorial cross is now badly weather beaten but fortunately a record was made in 1696 of the words. It was erected in memory of Eliseg, who annexed Powys from the Saxons, by his great-grandson Concenn. The pillar was broken by Cromwell's men and not re-erected until the 18th century.

A little further northwards the road from Llangollen curves round the spectacular **Horseshoe Pass** which affords remarkable views of the surrounding country. From the top of the pass can be seen the Vale of Clwyd and the ridge of Eglwyseg Rocks where Offa's Dyke path runs.

Just over a mile from Llangollen, at Pentrefelin, and nestling between the canal and the River Dee is the **Llangollen Motor Museum**. Many vehicles dating back over the ages are on display and the museum also has a parts department that stocks spares for old British cars. Occasionally Autojumbles are held there for the real enthusiasts. Ask at the museum for details and information concerning these events.

Found in the heart of the town, **The Sun Inn**, named by the local Llangollen brewery, is certainly a place not to be missed by lovers of beers and ales. Owned and personally run by Alan Adams and Paul Lamb, this pub is renowned throughout the area for its extensive range of real and unusual ales. As well as the six real ales that are always on tap, including the two local brews, Plassey Bitter and Cwrw Tudno, there is a long list of beers from around the world including Germany, Denmark, and Belgium.

The Sun Inn, Regent Street, Llangollen, Denbighshire LL20 8HN
Tel: 01978 860233

After selecting their pint from this superb choice, customers can then settle down in the comfortable surroundings of this charming late 18th-century building. During fine weather there is also the added delight of sitting out in the colourful, flower filled beer garden and, just in case, excellent beer and good company are not enough, Alan and Paul organise occasional entertainment and there are the jam sessions on Tuesdays to which all are invited.

At Old Flannel Mill, beside the fast flowing River Dee and just a mile from the centre of Llangollen, lies **The Old Mill Café and Bunkhouse**, owned and personally run by Jenny Broughton. Also the home of a popular canoe centre, the café does a roaring trade with those who enjoy the adventures of the water but also with those who appreciate delicious, home-cooked food. Open every day, from 08.30 until 18.00, the full menu of both hot and cold snacks and meals is supplemented by a list of daily

**The Old Mill Café and Bunkhouse, Mile End Mill, Berwyn Road
Llangollen, Denbighshire LL20 8AD Tel: 01978 869043**

specials that always prove popular. As well as the adjacent bunkhouse, also in the old mill building, bed and breakfast accommodation is available in a choice of three rooms, two of which have en-suite bathrooms. With excellent accommodation and delicious food available in this delightful location it is not surprising that the Old Mill Café and Bunkhouse is a popular choice for weekends and holidays. Following on from her success here, Jenny has taken over the Berwyn Arms at nearby Glyndyfrdwy, where further accommodation will soon be available.

Found high up in the hills, just a short drive from Llangollen, **Cefn-y-Fedw** is a delightful 16th-century stone farmhouse that has been fully modernised without losing any of its charm and character. Still the centre of a busy working farm, the house has been Shelagh Roberts' home since the 1970s and from here she has been providing superb bed and breakfast accommodation in two stylish, en-suite rooms. As well as breakfast, Shelagh is happy to provide evening meals and packed lunches by arrangement.

**Cefn-y-Fedw, near Panorama Walk, Garth Trevor, Llangollen
Denbighshire LL14 1UA Tel: 01978 823403**

However, whilst the cosy and friendly accommodation here is certainly outstanding it is the position of the house that makes Cefn-y-Fedw so idyllic. Set in a sheltered valley and surrounded by mature woodland, there is a wealth of wildlife right on the doorstep. Shelagh also has a qualification in Rural Tourism and is always happy to help guests and offer advice on the many interesting places, historical sites, and beautiful scenic spots in the surrounding countryside. Those looking for a relaxing holiday in the heart of the countryside should look no further than Cefn-y-Fedw.

WEST OF LLANGOLLEN

LLANTYSILIO   MAP 4 REF J5
1 mile W of Llangollen off A5

Situated on the banks of the River Dee **Llantysilio Church** has a brass plaque commemorating the fact that Robert Browning worshipped here in 1866. The brass was placed here by Lady Martin who is herself commemorated in a more modern chapel north of the choir.

The Sun Inn is set in the lush green hills of the beautiful Dee Valley and provides a lovely stopping-off point for visitors to the village of **Rhewl**, just northwest of Llantysilio. Alun Williams is the tenant of the inn which is owned by the Llantysilio Estate and has been a landlord in the area for 20 years. Open every day, and all day at the weekend, the public and lounge bars have a warm, cosy atmosphere which is enhanced by low, beamed ceilings and welcoming open log fires; one of the features of the

The Sun Inn, Rhewl, Denbighshire LL20 7YT
Tel: 01978 861043

inn, an old-fashioned range, is also lit on cold evenings. In these comfortable surroundings customers can savour real ales. The range on tap changes weekly, and includes Welsh lager, stouts, and draught dry cider. It should also be remembered that The Sun Inn was voted CAMRA pub of the year in 1997 for this area. The bar meals are both substantial and very reasonably priced; Alun cooks until 22.00 each evening. Children are welcome until 21.00 in all areas except the main bar and they will particularly enjoy the juke box and pool table housed in an adjacent building.

BRYNEGLWYS   MAP 4 REF I5
4 miles NW of Llangollen off A5104

Plas-Yn-Yale is the former home of the Yale family and birthplace of Elihu Yale's father. Elihu himself was born in 1649 in Boston, Massachusetts, and went on to become a governor in India before returning to England. Known for his philanthropy, he was approached by an American College who, after receiving generous help, named their new college in Newhaven after him. In 1745, 24 years after his death, the whole establishment was named Yale University. The nearby village church at Bryneglwys, high up on Llantysilio Mountain, has mementoes of his family.

Lying at the bottom of a long fox glove-lined drive, **Ty Cerrig Country Guest House** is a charming early 18th-century former farmhouse that incorporates a barn extension. The home of Elaine and Richard Price, this ceased to be a working farm in the 1970s and it is now a small holding with a large garden, surrounded by beautiful countryside in every direction. From this idyllic house, Elaine and Richard offer outstanding bed

Ty Cerrig Country Guest House, Bryneglwys, near Corwen, Denbighshire LL21 9NN Tel: 01490 450307

and breakfast accommodation in a choice of three excellent guest rooms. All are decorated and furnished with comfort in mind but also in a style that reflects the age of the building. Naturally, there are magnificent views from the bedroom windows and, downstairs, guests can not only enjoy Elaine's delicious home-cooking at breakfast and dinner (a popular option with many guests) but also soak up the atmosphere of this old house in the dining room, with its baker's oven, and in the cosy sitting room.

Despite being called **The New Inn**, this pub dates back to the early 1600s, although the rear of the building is a later addition. The owners, Joe and Bronwen Tango, met in New Zealand and besides helping Bronwen run the pub Joe, who is a Maori, also shears sheep throughout the country. This is a delightful and charming inn, which the couple, since coming here in 1994, have slowly refurbished to provide the cosy, olde worlde atmosphere that pervades today. Open every evening, for Sunday lunchtime throughout the year, for Saturday lunchtimes between Easter and the end of August and all day Bank Holiday Mondays, this pub has a well regarded reputation locally for excellent ales and delicious food and it is well worth making the effort to find.

**The New Inn, Bryneglwys, Denbighshire LL21 9LP
Tel: 01490 450254**

With Bronwen and Joe sharing the culinary work, the interesting and extensive menu is very much a mix of flavours and tastes and culminates each year with a Hangi, a traditional Maori feast that is usually held in August. For those visiting the area, the couple also offer self-catering accommodation in a cottage opposite the pub. Available all year round, the comfortable and well furnished cottage sleeps six and, of course, there is the pub close by for those not willing to cook. (The New Inn is open on other lunchtimes only by prior arrangement for party bookings.)

CORWEN   MAP 4 REF I5
8 miles W of Llangollen on A5

This market town was once the headquarters of Owain Glyndwr, who gathered his forces here before entering into his various campaigns. The church, parts of which date from the 13th century, has an incised dagger in a lintel of the doorway which is known as **Glyndwr's Sword**. It was reputedly made by Glyndwr when he threw a dagger from the hill above in a fit of rage against the townsfolk. The dagger mark, in fact, dates from the 7th-9th centuries and there is another such mark on a 12th-century cross outside the southwest corner of the church.

Across the river from the town lies **Caer Derwyn**, a stone rampart around a hill which dates from Roman times. Also found close by, set in beautiful countryside to the northwest of Corwen, is **Rug Chapel**, a rare example of a private 17th-century chapel. Little changed since it was founded by 'Old Blue Stocking' Colonel William Salusbury, the plain exterior gives no clues to the exquisitely decorated interior. Few parts of the chapel are left unadorned and, as well as the beautifully carved rood screen, the ceiling beams are painted with rose motifs.

The Eagles Hotel, standing in The Square right in the heart of the town, is a charming 18th-century coaching inn that still has the stables to the rear of the inn. Through the years, the hotel has been very much part of life in Corwen and, in the mid-19th century, it was also used for the

The Eagles Hotel, The Square, Corwen, Denbighshire LL21 0DG
Tel: 01490 413280

fortnightly meetings of the workhouse guardians: at that time the hire of the room cost the guardians just £4 per annum. Today, the inn is managed by Maria and Steve Carlile and, though the workhouse guardians no longer meet here, it is still a popular place for the locals to catch up on the news. With a full range of drinks behind the bar and a very pleasant atmosphere, this is certainly a super place for a relaxing drink and a chat.

Corwen Manor, found on the main road through the town, is not, as its name would suggest, an old gentleman's residence, but a Victorian workhouse that has been restored and renovated and now houses a variety of crafts shops and a café, as well as having bed and breakfast accommodation. Planned and constructed by the Workhouse Guardians, who met fortnightly at the nearby Eagles Hotel, the workhouse was completed in 1840 with room to take in 150 paupers of the seven parishes of the surrounding area. Since the dark days of the poorhouse, the building has seen many uses including both an engineering factory and a shirt-

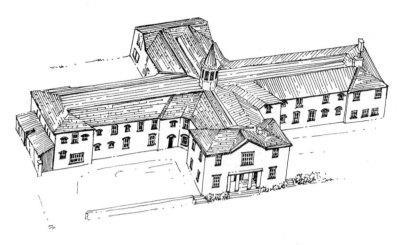

Corwen Manor, 8 London Road, Corwen, Denbighshire LL21 0DR
Tel: 01490 413196

making factory. Although awarded the status of a Listed Building of historic and architectural interest, the building had, by 1979, fallen into a great state of disrepair and was only saved from demolition by the Orissor Trust. Following extensive rebuilding, the Sayer family purchased the property in 1989 and, as well as changing the name to Corwen Manor, they began to secure the building's future by first opening the bed and breakfast accommodation.

Today, visitors to Corwen Manor, can not only enjoy the services of the Candle Workshop but also watch the candles being made and play a round of crazy golf. There are also two cafés, one non-smoking and the other for smokers, and a superb craft shop stocked with all manner of interesting and unusual items and gifts, including candle making equipment and knitting wools.

Situated at **Betws Gwerfil Goch**, in the valley of the River Alwyn and just four miles northwest of Corwen, lies **Delfryn**, the delightful home of Lesley and Frank Hart. The couple moved here from Cumbria in the spring of 1997 and, after completely refurbishing this charming old house, they are now offering superb country house bed and breakfast accommodation in three magnificent en-suite guest rooms. Each room is individually decorated and furnished in the same stylish manner as the rest of Delfryn and from many of the windows there are glorious views over the gentle Denbighshire countryside. The delicious home-cooked breakfast and evening meals are taken in the wonderful wooden panelled dining room where all the guests sit around the large, old oak table. With no televisions to distract guests, the evening conversations can certainly be a

**Delfryn, Betws Gwerfil Goch, near Corwen, Denbighshire LL21 9PU
Tel: 01490 460387**

highlight of the day. As well as spending a great deal of time and care on the house, Lesley and Frank have also paid attention to the large, secluded garden. Here they have planted over 1,000 trees and shrubs to create not only a real wildlife garden but also an interesting nature trail for guests to enjoy.

LLANDRILLO
11 miles W of Llangollen on B4401

MAP 4 REF I5

The road to Llandrillo, from the north, follows the Vale of Edeirion and the River Dee as it weaves its way below the northwest slopes of the **Berwyn Mountains**, another mountain range that is popular with walkers and visitors. This small village is a good starting point for walks in the Berwyns; footpaths from the village lead towards **Craig Berwyn** summit which is over 2,100 feet high.

Between Llandrillo and nearby Corwen lies **Llangar Church**, a small medieval building which overlooks the confluence of the Rivers Dee and Alwen. Fortunately, though the church was superseded in the mid 19th century it has retained many of its ancient features including the extensive 15th-century wall paintings and minstrels' gallery.

GLYNDYFRDWY
3 miles W of Llangollen on A5

MAP 4 REF I5

Once the estate of Owain Glyndwr, this village lies on the main A5 road between the Berwyn and the Llantysilio mountains. A mound by the road, known as **Owain Glyndwr's Mound**, is believed to have been the site of his manor. The village is now home of 'The Original Butterfly Man' a craft workshop full of ornamental butterflies that can be seen adorning homes across the country.

Found just west of Glyndyfrdwy, at **Carrog**, and with a magnificent view overlooking the River Dee, **The Grouse Inn** is a charming early 19th-century farmhouse that became a public house at the turn of the century. A finalist for the Pub of the Year Award, this attractive inn has much to

**The Grouse Inn, Carrog, near Corwen, Denbighshire LL21 9AT
Tel: 01490 430272**

offer the visitor apart from its wonderful hospitality. Run by Sarah Kenrick, The Grouse Inn is open every day, from noon onwards, to provide its customers with fine food and drink. As well as the wonderful range of Lees ales that are served here, there is also a delicious menu of ever changing dishes that are sure to find favour with everyone. However, for those who wish to exercise their 'little grey cells' there is a popular quiz night every Wednesday and the occasional singer provides the entertainment mid-week. For those who find The Grouse Inn during pleasant weather, there is also a pretty patio area from which not only can the river be seen but also the delightful steam trains of the Llangollen Railway.

EAST OF LLANGOLLEN

CEFN-MAWR   Map 4 ref J5
5 miles E of Llangollen on B5605

Pontcysyllte, built by Thomas Telford in 1805, is an amazing aqueduct

Pontcysyllte Aqueduct, Cefn-mawr

that carries the Shropshire Union Canal across the River Dee, some 126 feet below. The magnificent construction is some 1,007 feet long and, despite scorn from people at the time of its building, this cast iron trough supported by 18 stone pillars is still regularly used by pleasure boats.

RUABON   MAP 4 REF J5
7 miles E of Llangollen off B5605

This partly industrial town lies at the entrance to the picturesque Vale of Llangollen and has strong links with the historically omnipotent Wynnstay family.

Tucked away in Duke Street, is the attractive and distinctive **Duke of Wellington**, an early 19th-century inn part of which was also the village shop. Since moving here in Spring 1998, Mary and Eddie Potts and their daughter Sarah have worked hard to turn around the fortunes of this pub which was very near closing for good. Today, their efforts have been rewarded as the pub is fast becoming one of the most popular places for fine food and drink in the area. The charming exterior of this beautiful Georgian building is mirrored inside where, after a full refurbishment, a cosy and relaxing atmosphere has been created that is sure to suit all customers. As well as serving a good range of well kept beers, ales, and lagers, The Duke of Wellington also has a fine reputation for its traditional home-cooked meals, including the all day breakfast, that are served at both

**The Duke of Wellington, Duke Street, Ruabon, Wrexham LL14 6DE
Tel: 01978 820381**

lunchtimes and in the evening. Add to this the three excellent guest rooms and the pleasant, rear beer garden and it is easy to see why the pub has become so popular.

BERSHAM   Map 4 ref J5
8 miles NE of Llangollen off A483

Part of the **Clywedog Valley and Trail** that skirts around the south and west of Wrexham and includes several places of industrial interest, Bersham was established around 1670 and was home to the Davis brothers. The fine workmanship of the famous iron master brothers can be seen in the beautiful gates at Chirk Park and at St Giles' Church in Wrexham. Its master and owner from 1762, John 'Iron Mad' Wilkinson, is known for the cannons he bored for use in the American War of Independence and also for the cylinders he produced for James Watt's steam engines. Today, the 18th-century ironworks are now formally the **Bersham Ironworks and Heritage Centre** and it has been developed to give an informative insight into the history of this once busy industrial area.

MINERA   Map 4 ref J4
7 miles NE of Llangollen off A525

This old lead mine in the village is now an informative and enjoyable tourist attraction on the Clywedog trail where demonstrations of how lead was mined and its effect upon those working in the industry are shown.

Not far from Minera is **Nant Mill**, a countryside centre that has educational displays which include a man-sized mole tunnel. There are also marked nature trails which follow parts of this industrious valley.

PONCIAU   MAP 4 REF J5
8 miles E of Llangollen off B5605

Found just to the north of Ruabon in the village of **Ponciau** and dating back over 100 years, **The Cross Keys** is very much the village pub, a place for the locals to come to for a relaxing drink after a hard day's work. Traditionally decorated and furnished, the pub is run by Brian Bassett and it

The Cross Keys, Australia Street, Ponciau, Wrexham LL14 1ED
Tel: 01978 840458

is thanks to him and his staff that the atmosphere here is both warm and welcoming. A fine selection of well-kept ales are served behind the bar and, it is for this, and the chance to catch up on the local gossip that draws people here. Open every day and all day on Fridays and Saturdays, those looking for a traditional pub will certainly find that The Cross Keys fits the bill.

SOUTH OF LLANGOLLEN

GLYNCEIRIOG   MAP 4 REF J5
2 miles S of Llangollen on B4500

This former slate mining village is home to the **Chwarel Wynne Slate Caverns and Museum**. As well as telling the story of the industry that once supported the village, there is also a guided tour of the caverns and a nature trail around the surrounding area. Lying in the secluded Vale of Ceiriog, this is a beautiful district of wooded hills which reach westwards towards Bala and offer surprisingly pastoral views and vistas.

Situated within its own landscaped grounds and on high ground overlooking the beautiful Ceiriog Valley, the **Plas Owen Hotel** is a hidden treasure well worth seeking out. The hotel was built in this delightful position in 1980 by the Owen family and today it is personally run by Sarah and Stephen Owen. Open all year round and with 17 superb ensuite guest rooms, the Plas Owen Hotel has excellent facilities and is happy to accommodate families, children, and the pet dog.

**Plas Owen Hotel, Glyn Ceiriog, near Llangollen
Wrexham LL20 7DE Tel: 01691 718707 Fax: 01691 718794**

The hotel is also well known locally for its spacious Berwyn restaurant, which is open to non-residents, and serves a delicious mixture of traditional and continental cuisine. Before dinner, hotel residents can enjoy a drink and a chat with other guests in their private bar or join the locals in the Lounge bar, where, quite often, there is Welsh singing. This is the ideal location for a relaxing holiday, where not only is there plenty to see and do in the surrounding area but also guests can sit on the sunny outdoor patio and take in the fresh air, the sounds of the bubbling stream nearby, and just enjoy the view.

LLANARMON DYFFRYN CEIRIOG   MAP 4 REF I6
6 miles S of Llangollen on B4500

This peaceful village, in the heart of the Vale of Ceiriog, was the birthplace of the famous Welsh bard, Ceiriog (John Hughes). From here there are guided hill walks arranged at 'Gwynfa' by the school in the village.

CHIRK   MAP 4 REF J5
6 miles SE of Llangollen off A5

This attractive border town's origins lie in the 11th-century castle of which, unfortunately, little remains. It is now perhaps better known for the National Trust owned **Chirk Castle** which lies just two miles from the town. Chirk Castle was begun in the late 13th century on land granted by Edward

Chirk Castle

I to Roger de Mortimer. Entering the parkland through magnificent wrought iron gates made by the Davis brothers of Bersham visitors head towards the still inhabited castle. Although it has been rebuilt on various occasions over the years, the structure is still fairly impressive. Its interior has various styles that reflect the continual changes through the ages whilst the parkland contains attractive gardens and from the lake to the north of the castle part of Offa's Dyke can be seen.

The Myddleton family, who have occupied the castle since 1595, have a red hand on their coat of arms. Legend has it that the bloody hand appears there as a reminder of the family's past misdeeds and could not be removed until a prisoner had survived 10 years in the castle dungeons.

8 North Powys

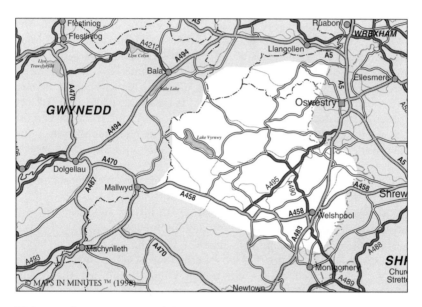

This northern section of Powys, once part of the old county of Montgomeryshire, is an area of varied landscape and small towns and villages. Situated between the high lands of Snowdonia in the west and the farmlands of Shropshire in the east, this is a gentle and pleasant region through which many rivers and streams make their way.

Water plays an important part in the life of north Powys and it is home to the highest waterfall outside Scotland, Pistyll Rhaeadr as well as Lake Vyrnwy. Built in the 1880s to supply the expanding city of Liverpool with water, this large reservoir is not only famous for its splendid feats of Victorian engineering but also as a location for the film *The Dambusters*.

The major settlement here is Welshpool, a town situated on the banks of the River Severn that is also close to the English border. Originally known as Pool, the prefix was added to ensure that the dispute regarding its nationality was finalised once and for all. From the town leisurely canal boat trips can be taken along the Montgomery Canal but there is also a narrow gauge steam railway running westwards to Llanfair Caereinion. Near the town can also be found the splendid National Trust property, Powis Castle, that is famous for its magnificent gardens and the treasures housed with the mansion.

WELSHPOOL

This is a bustling market town which was granted a charter in 1263 by the Prince of Powys. For a long time the town was known as 'Pool', the Welsh prefix being added in 1835 to settle the long running dispute about its location on the borders with England. Welshpool has several examples of old architecture, the half timbered structure near the town hall being one of many. The **Powysland Museum**, housed in a former warehouse beside the Montgomery Canal, was founded by Morris Jones in 1874. Earlier, many of the artefacts that first formed the museum's collection had been put together by the Powysland Club - a group of Victorian gentlemen interested in the history of mid Wales. There are several aspects to this museum, the development of life in Montgomeryshire from the earliest settlers to the 20th century; displays of farming equipment; collections telling the story of the building of first the canals and then the railways; and also some of the remains of Strata Marcella. Founded in around 1170 by Owain Cyfeiliog, Prince of Powys, for Cistercian monks, the abbey was razed to the ground during the Reformation.

Along with the museum, the old warehouse is also home to the **Montgomery Canal Centre**, which, along with other exhibits, tells the story of the waterway. Completed in 1821, the canal carried coal and food from Welshpool to the upper reaches of the River Severn. Though, as with other canals, its decline came with the growth in the railways, the section of the canal at Welshpool is open for pleasure cruises.

The town is also home to two other interesting buildings, the **Cockpit** and **Grace Evans' Cottage**. The only surviving cockpit on its original site in Wales, this venue for the bloodthirsty sport was built in the 18th century and remained in use until the sport was banned in Britain in 1849. Grace Evans is certainly one of Welshpool's best known citizens as she was instrumental in rescuing Lord Nithsdale from the Tower of London in 1716. Grace, Lady Nithsdale's maid, fled with the couple to France but she returned to Welshpool in 1735 and lived at the cottage, reputedly given to her by a grateful Lord Nithsdale, until her death three years later.

Perhaps best known in the area, however, is **Powis Castle**, just one mile southwest of Welshpool. The castle has been inhabited for around 500 years and subsequent alterations have been made which give the building the look of a mansion rather than a castle. The remains of a Norman motte and bailey are thought to be from the original castle which is believed to have been built in the early 12th century and was destroyed during a dispute between Llewelyn the Great and Gruffydd ap Gwenwynwyn, a local landowner. Edward I granted the family a barony on condition that they renounced their Welsh titles which they subsequently did and thus the present castle was begun. It was defended for the royalist cause in the Civil War but fell to Parliament in 1644.

Powis Castle, Welshpool

Changing hands several times over the centuries, Powis reflects the tastes of the various owners over the centuries which have included Edward Clive, son of Clive of India. Amongst many other riches the castle is home to the **Clive Museum** which features treasures from the famous man's time in India. The fine, wooded grounds and terraced gardens which include the original statues, an orangery and aviary, constructed in the 18th century, all complement the castle's situation. Powis Castle was eventually given to the National Trust in 1952 and makes a very interesting visit for those curious about the various aspects of history and influence in the area.

Just a mile or so from Welshpool and in a magnificent, elevated position is **Tynllwyn Farm** with its impressive farmhouse that dates from 1861. This has been the home of Freda and Ivor Emberton since the 1950s and, though this is a working beef cattle and sheep farm, visitors who take advantage of the couple's superb bed and breakfast accommodation will see little of the daily farm workings. This grand Victorian farmhouse, of mellow red brick, has been modernised to provide the comforts and conveniences of late 20th-century living without taking away the grandeur and charm of the Victorian's style. The well proportioned rooms are all delightfully decorated and furnished and the atmosphere is that of a family home. There is a range of bedroom accommodation and children of any age are welcome. A delicious farmhouse breakfast awaits guests each

Tynllwyn Farm, Welshpool, Powys SY21 9BW
Tel: 01938 553175/553054

morning and home-cooked evening meals are available by arrangement. As Tynllwyn Farm has become recognised over the years as one of the best establishments of its kind in the area, (one look at the visitor's book will confirm this) booking early is essential to avoid disappointment.

NORTH OF WELSHPOOL

GUILSFIELD   MAP 4 REF J7
4 miles N of Welshpool on B4392

The 15th-century village church here is well worth a second glance as not only does it have an unusual upper chamber above the south porch but also a splendid panelled roof and some 19th-century vaulting.

The Oak Inn in the centre of the village is hard to miss as it is an impressive early 18th-century black-and-white building. Managed by Diane and Peter Galley, the interior of the excellent pub is as traditional and

**The Oak Inn, Guilsfield, Powys SY21 9NH
Tel: 01938 553391**

inviting as the exterior would suggest and the atmosphere created by the charming hosts is equally welcoming. Those looking for tasty food as well as a delicious, refreshing pint, should not be put off by the village's old Welsh name, Cegidfa, which means a place abounding in hemlock, as The Oak Inn is the place to come. As well as the wide range of ales and beers available at the bar, the menu of bar snacks and meals is sure to include everyone's favourite dish. Children too are well catered for at the Oak Inn as there is a superb outdoor play area.

LLANSANTFFRAID-YM-MECHAIN   Map 4 ref J6
10 miles N of Welshpool on A495

This large border village, in the valley of the River Vyrnwy, has a church with a fine Jacobean window dating from 1619.

In a beautiful, south-facing, elevated position, overlooking the village and with magnificent views of the Vyrnwy and Cain valleys, lies **Penygarreg**. This charming 17th-century longhouse, situated amid 10 acres of grounds which include a lovely bluebell wood, has been Mona Mills' home since the late 1960s and, for the past few years, she has been offering superb bed and breakfast accommodation with the help of her friend Doreen. Though the house is old, it has been carefully adapted to the requirements of modern living but its old world charm has certainly not been lost along the way. The upstairs rooms, including the three guest rooms, all retain their original exposed beams and the guest rooms have all, like the rest of the house, been furnished and decorated for guests' comfort and convenience. There is an equally charming lounge, complete with a piano, and the dining room overlooks the idyllic cottage garden. Many of the delicious home-cooked foods and wonderful home-made preserves are provided from the garden and they, along with the warm and

**Penygarreg, Winllan Road, Llansantffraid-ym-Mechain
Powys SY22 6TS Tel: 01691 828452 Fax: 01691 648070**

friendly atmosphere at Penygarreg, help to make it one of the most enjoyable places to stay in the area.

LLANGEDWYN   Map 4 ref J6
12 miles N of Welshpool on B4396

Not far from this village, close to the English border, lies one of Wales' most nationalistic shrines, **Sycarth Castle Mound**. This grassy mound marks the site of one of Owain Glyndwr's courts, reputedly a grand palace with nine great halls. The shrine was immortalised by Bard Iolo Goch as a place of 'no want, no hunger, no shame, No-one is ever thirsty at Sycarth'.

LLANRHAEADR YM MOCHNANT   Map 4 ref I6
14 miles NW of Welshpool on B4396

Despite its relative isolation this village attracts many visitors who come through on their way to **Pistyll Rhaeadr** which lies about three and a half miles from the village down a narrow lane. One of the Seven Wonders of Wales and with a drop of 240 feet, this is the highest waterfall south of the Scottish Highlands. Translated the names means Spout Waterfall, an obvious name as the water drops vertically before running through a natural tunnel in the rock before reappearing again. There is parking close by and a footpath leads towards the 2,713 feet summit of **Moel Sych**.

As was once common in the area, Llanrhaeadr ym Mochnant still maintains the plygeiniau, a form of Christmas carol service. Groups of men wander from church to church where they give unaccompanied performances of Welsh carols.

LLANGYNOG
17 miles NW of Welshpool on B4391

Situated where the Rivers Tanat and Eirth meet, the village's name recalls Cynog, the son of the 5th-century prince, Brychan. Lead and slate were once extracted from the surrounding hills but exhaustion and flooding has seen to their demise.

Further up the River Tanat, in the hamlet of **Pennant Melangell** lies **St Melangell's Church**, where, inside, are two images, one said to be of a Welsh prince and the other of the 7th-century St Melangell. The story goes that a hunted hare took refuge in the saint's cloak and, thus, she became patron saint of hares which were once treated as sacred in the area. A short distance away from the church the valley ends in a small waterfall.

LLANFYLLIN   MAP 4 REF I6
12 miles N of Welshpool on A490

This charming and peaceful hillside town lies in the valley of the River Cain and is home to **St Myllin's Well**. Water from the well has, from the 6th century, been thought to cure all manner of ailments and certainly the view from the well, over the town and to the Berwyn Mountains beyond, is uplifting.

WEST OF WELSHPOOL

MEIFOD   MAP 4 REF I7
6 miles NW of Welshpool on A495

The pretty village of Meifod is remembered in Welsh literature as being the location of the summer residence of the princes of Powys. The village church has an interesting 9th-century gravestone with an old Christian symbol marked on it.

Beneath Dyffryn Hill and very near the popular Glyndwr's Way lies **Pentre-Gôf Farm** which has been in Job Watkin's family for centuries. The outstanding farmhouse, which dates back to the early 16th century, is a beautiful listed building that is constructed in the traditional lattice and mortar style. From this exceptional home, Job and his wife Sheila have been offering superb bed and breakfast accommodation in two magnificent en-suite rooms. The interior of this large farmhouse is very much in keeping with the age of the building, though there are also the modern conveniences of the late 20th century, and the guest rooms are similarly decorated and furnished. Breakfast, and dinner if arranged, is taken at an ancient 14 foot long solid oak table in a charming beamed room that was

Pentre-Gôf Farm, Meifod, Powys SY22 6DH
Tel: 01938 500353

once the farm's milk house and parlour. Those lucky enough to find a
room available at Pentre-Gôf will not only enjoy this out-of-this-world
house and setting but also the warm and friendly hospitality that Sheila
and Job extend to all their guests.

Situated in the tiny hamlet of **Pont Robert** just west of Meifod, **The
Royal Oak Inn** is a superb pub that is well worth taking the time to find.

The Royal Oak Inn, Pont Robert, near Meifod, Powys SY22 6HY
Tel: 01938 500243

Dating back to the late 1700s, this lovely old inn was purchased by Joyce Evans in 1993 and, looking at the magnificent building today, it is hard to believe that before the sale the inn had been standing empty for two years. The massive refurbishment that was necessary has not hidden but highlighted the age of this lovely building and only increased the friendly and comfortable atmosphere that Joyce has created. The perfect place for a pint or two of one of the range of well-kept real ales from the bar, The Royal Oak also serves a tantalising menu of delicious bar snacks and meals throughout the day. With its charming, secluded beer garden, this is the ideal place for all the family and those looking for overnight accommodation are also very well looked after with a choice of three excellent guest rooms as well as the bunkroom. Not surprisingly, The Royal Oak Inn has become a popular place and any one who makes their way here will not be disappointed.

LLANWDDYN   MAP 4 REF H7
14 miles W of Welshpool on B4393

The village lies at the southern end of **Lake Vyrnwy** (Llyn Efyrnwy), a four mile stretch of water dammed at its southern end in 1886-90 to feed the demands of Liverpool. Close to the dam, which is 390 yards long, 144 feet high, and a splendid testament to Victorian engineering, is a monument that marks the start of the **Hirnant Tunnel**. This two mile long tunnel is the first stage of a 75 mile aqueduct carrying the water to Liverpool. A road circumnavigates the lake but a walk of roughly 14 miles around the lake, which is dotted with picnic spots, can be made.

The first of the massive reservoirs that have been constructed in north and mid Wales, the original village of Llanwddyn, home to some 400 people, was flooded in its building. The reservoir's visitor centre not only tells the story of the construction but it is also home to an RSPB centre. The

Lake Vyrnwy

society oversees an estate of 16,000 acres where you might be fortunate to see some unusual birds such as the crossbill or redpoll. Those visiting the lake may find it familiar as it was used as a location for the film *The Dambusters*.

Situated in the Montgomeryshire Hills at Hirnant, just northwest of Llanwddyn, and near to Lake Vyrnwy, **Blaen Hirnant Guest House** occupies a superb position, with fine views of the surrounding hills and some excellent walking country right on the door step. This attractive 14th-century house, of a cruck beam design, was bought by June and John Russell in 1990 and, after spending a year completely refurbishing the property, they now have a fantastic family home. This charming couple

**Blaen Hirnant Guest House, Hirnant, near Pen-y-Bont Fawr
Powys SY10 0HR Tel: 01691 870330**

also have three comfortable en-suite guest rooms, one of the which is on the ground floor. As with the rest of the house, many of the original building's features have been retained and, upstairs, not only can the cruck beams still be seen but a wall has been left exposed to show the wattle and daub construction. However, guests' comfort has not been forgotten and there is everything the holidaymaker could wish for to make them feel truly at home. Along the peace and quiet of this tucked away location, Blaen Hirnant - the name means source of the long river - offers guests delicious home-cooking for breakfast and, if arranged, dinner in the evening. The guest house is open from mid January to mid December but, unfortunately, it is not suitable for young children.

Set alongside the main road at **Foel**, just south of Llanwddyn, **The Dyffryn Restaurant** is a delightful establishment that has been owned by Mandy Jones since 1991 though she has worked here for many years. A

The Dyffryn Restaurant, Foel, Powys SY21 0NR
Tel: 01938 820214

self-taught cook, Mandy opens the restaurant most days in the summer and certainly Fridays and the weekends. By day, this is a charming tea rooms, where all manner of tasty, home-cooked dishes are available, all day, but, in the evening, the mood and the menu changes for dinner. Fully licensed and with a delicious choice of dishes from which to choose, those coming here for dinner will receive the same warm welcome and genuine home-cooking as the day time visitors. Well known locally, The Dyffryn Restaurant is popular and well frequented whatever the time of day. Visitors to the area might also be interested to learn that Mandy offers comfortable bed and breakfast in three rooms found on the first floor of the main house which is adjacent to the superb dining room. As well decorated and furnished as the restaurant, guests can enjoy a relaxed night's sleep with the welcome of the superb breakfast when they awake.

LLANFAIR CAEREINION
8 miles W of Welshpool on B4389

MAP 4 REF I7

Once a centre for flannel manufacture, this small town is the terminus for another of Wales' restored steam railways.

When the **Welshpool and Llanfair Railway** line first opened, in 1903, there were great local celebrations because, as early as 1845, schemes and proposals for such a route had been put forward but work did not eventually start until 1901. This light railway, taking trains packed with passengers each market day, ran successfully until the passenger service ended in the 1920s. Now reopened, visitors can take an enjoyable trip along the route

**Welshpool and Llanfair Railway, The Station, Llanfair Caereinion
Powys SY21 0SF Tel: 01938 810441**

in restored rolling stock pulled by one of the line's steam engines with
both a driver and a fireman on board. The station at Llanfair Caereinion is
not only a suitable place to begin the journey but there is also a shop and
goods shed here that dates from 1903. Travelling along the banks of the
River Banwy as far as Cyfronydd station, the line cross the river via a three
span bridge before taking in the Brynelin Viaduct to cross the deep valley
of the Cwmbaw stream. **Castle Caereinion**, approximately the halfway
point of the journey, is the perfect stopping point for a picnic and a visit
to this charming rural hamlet. From here the track climbs steeply to the
halt at Golfa, a siding once used for sheep and coal, before climbing once
again to the destination, Welshpool. This is a marvellous way to see the
local countryside and there are also numerous buildings of interest along
the route.

SOUTH OF WELSHPOOL

MARTON   MAP 4 REF J8
4 miles S of Welshpool on B4386

Separated from Welshpool by Long Mountain, this pretty village lies right
on the border with England.

The magnificent **Lowfield Inn** is a charming 300-year-old building that
was originally a farmhouse before becoming an alehouse. As well as re-

taining its thatched roof, this attractive white building is decorated with a mass of colourful hanging baskets and window boxes in summer and, surrounded by such glorious countryside, the well maintained beer garden is certainly a picturesque spot in which to sit and enjoy the delights of the inn. Personally run by Bernie and Babs Collins, The Lowfield Inn is as

**The Lowfield Inn, Marton, near Welshpool, Powys SY21 8JK
Tel: 01743 891313**

cosy and characterful inside as the exterior would suggest: there are low ceilings, a large stone fireplace, and a display of old prints of the property through the years. A fine selection of real ales, with an ever changing guest beer, as well as the usual lagers and stouts, are served from the bar and food is also available at both lunchtime and in the evening.

Babs is the chef of the partnership and the comprehensive menu of tasty dishes she creates is complemented by a choice of daily specials. For top quality food and drink, in a pleasant and friendly atmosphere The Lowfield Inn certainly takes some beating. However, this is not all that Bernie and Babs have to offer their customers as, opposite the inn, they have a touring caravan and camping site with a mix of hard and soft pitches. All the usual facilities are provided and the setting is near perfect, with the rolling countryside all around and the wonderful inn across the road.

BERRIEW   MAP 4 REF J8
4 miles S of Welshpool on B4385

Over the years, this picturesque village of half-timbered houses has won the 'best kept village' award. Berriew is associated with St Beuno where, it is recalled, he apparently heard English voices whilst communing by the River Severn and thus warned the villagers of this pagan threat. The village is also the home of the **Andrew Logan Museum of Sculpture**, an interesting gallery of modern British work. Certainly fascinating to view, Andrew Logan was the man behind the Alternative Miss World Contest, begun in the 1970s, and some of the fantastic costumes from the contest are also on display.

Situated on the banks of the River Severn, with gentle rolling hills in the background, **Glansevern Hall Gardens** have been developed by Jenny and Neville Thomas into a wonderful and interesting place to visit for all the family. The couple purchased the early 19th-century Glansevern Hall in 198 and since then they have added a vast collection of new plants and species to the already laid out grounds of the house. Covering some 15 acres, mostly on level ground, there are several different areas that have

Glansevern Hall Gardens, Berriew, near Welshpool, Powys SY21 8AH
Tel: 01686 640200 Fax: 01686 640829

been carefully designed to show the myriad of plants here in their best locations. Water plays an important part in any garden and, as well as the lakeside walk through mixed woodland with its colourful displays of bulbs in early spring, there is a striking water garden. Beside tumbling streams that make their way into the lake, a whole range of water-loving plants flourish throughout the spring and summer.

The original rock garden, first laid out in 1840, has been replanted but in a manner in keeping with the extravagance of the Victorian gardeners. Nearer to the house are the more traditional herbaceous borders and beds and, one of the favourites of all, a charming rose garden with both new and old varieties. In the old converted stables, visitors have the opportunity to purchase a souvenir of their visit as there are many plants on sale, all of which have been grown at Glansevern. Here too is a cosy tea room, serving all manner of home-made cakes and pastries, and also a garden shop stocked full of interesting items, many of which are locally made.

At **Garthmyl**, just south of Berriew, and ideally situated as a base from which to tour the delights of Powys, lies **Tanyfron Farm** the perfect place

Tanyfron Farm, Garthmyl, near Montgomery, Powys SY15 6RZ
Tel: 01686 640297

for a family holiday. This attractive farmhouse was once a pub, called the Highway Inn and, those who visit it will not be surprised to learn, it is also a listed building. Of solid red brick and with charming Gothic windows, the farmhouse is the home of Syliva and Roy Matthews, in fact, Roy has lived on this sheep and suckler beef farm all his life. Since 1980, the couple have also been offering comfortable and friendly bed and breakfast accommodation in two cosy yet spacious rooms. Not only can guests expect to have a relaxing and peaceful stay here but there is also the promise of a hearty home-cooked breakfast each morning and, by prior arrangement, Syliva and Roy also provide packed lunches and an evening meal.

9 Mid Powys

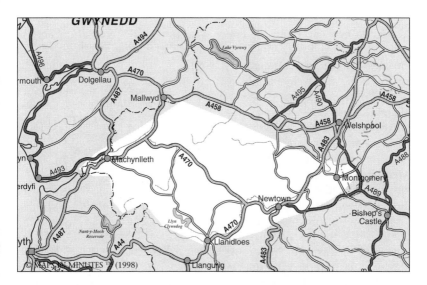

This final area of north and mid Wales stretches from the English border, across the country, to the coast and Cardigan Bay. A diverse and also sparsely populated region, to the east are the pretty, rural border villages and, to the west, the old lead mining communities on the southern side of the Dyfi estuary.

Montgomery, a tiny anglicized town that gave its name to the county of Montgomeryshire, not only has a splendidly situated ruined castle but it is also close to some of the best preserved sections of Offa's Dyke. Nearby Newtown, which despite its name was founded in the 10th century, is another interesting and historic market town that is also the home of the famous High Street newsagents, WH Smith. The associated museum tells of the company's growth from its humble beginnings in 1792 and those who are interested in history, particularly social history, will find the Robert Owen Memorial Museum well worth a visit.

To the west, beyond the quaint town of Llanidloes, lies Machynlleth, the home of Owain Glyndwr's Parliament in the 15th century. A visit to the Welsh hero's centre, which is found in the part 15th century parliament house, tells the story of Glyndwr and his struggle against the English. By way of a contrast, the town is the home of the Welsh Museum of Modern Art.

Finally, there is the Dyfi estuary, once a centre of iron smelting that is now a popular place with holiday makers as well as ornithologists who come to see the wealth of birds that feed on the mudflats and marshes left by the retreating tide.

NEWTOWN

The name, here, is certainly deceptive as the town's origins date from around AD 973 but Newtown came to prominence after being granted a charter by Edward I in 1280. It became a cen-tre for textiles and weaving and, by the 19th century, the home of the Welsh flannel industry. Newton was also the birthplace of Robert Owen (1771-1858), a reformer and founder of the cooperative movement who lobbied vigorously for improved working con-ditions within the textile industry. The **Robert Owen Memorial Museum** on Broad Street reconstructs the story of his life whilst the **Textile Museum** tells the story of this once important in-dustry. A visit to the museum gives a very good idea of the working condi-tions that Robert Owen devoted much of his life to changing. His tomb lies

Tomb of Robert Owen, Newtown

in the churchyard of **St Mary's Church**. Abandoned in 1856 as it was too small and liable to flooding, St Mary's Church was restored in 1939.

St Mary's Church, Newtown

Another interesting visit to consider whilst in Newtown is the **WH Smith Museum**. The shop has been restored to its original 1927 layout and devotes much of its space to the history of the booksellers from 1792 onwards.

Ideally located in the heart of the town, in the Ladywell Shopping Precinct, **Jay's Restaurant** is the perfect place to call in for a mid-morning snack or a lunchtime treat. Personally run since 1992 by twins Ann and Carol, with the help of Ann's husband, John, the atmosphere here is warm and friendly with pine tables and chairs enhancing the country-kitchen

**Jay's Restaurant, Ladywell Shopping Precinct, Newtown
Powys SY16 1AF Tel: 01686 625395**

style of the restaurant. The mouth-watering menu is extensive and varied, with the emphasis on good wholesome cooking, and includes a selection of vegetarian dishes. With everything freshly prepared on the premises and using only the choicest produce, it is not surprising that Jay's Restaurant is a popular and busy central meeting place. However, during quieter moments John may be persuaded to tell of his former life as a valet to Prince Philip. Jay's is open all day from Monday to Saturday and is licensed.

In the heart of Newtown lies **The Pheasant Inn**, a friendly, popular pub that has been run, since 1993 by Jean Wareing and her friend Mona. Though the pub is by no means old, it was built in 1936 on the site of a

**The Pheasant Inn, Market Street, Newtown, Powys SY16 2PQ
Tel: 01686 625966**

former inn, it certainly does not lack in atmosphere which is provided by these two charming ladies and the delightful surroundings they have created. With an emphasis on excellent real ales, there is a good selection from the bar as well as the usual beers, lagers, and ciders, and for those who feel peckish, sandwiches are also available. Entertainment in the form of super league darts, pool, and dominoes is another well regarded aspect of the pub and, for use in fine weather, there is a pretty hidden patio beer garden to the rear of the premises. However, Jean and Mona's excellent hospitality does not end there as they also offer comfortable bed and breakfast accommodation in a choice of three rooms to which children are also welcome.

Standing on the main road west out of Newtown, though only minutes from the town centre, **The Flying Shuttle** is easily missed as it is surrounded by trees. However, it is certainly worth keeping an eye open for this modern pub as visitors can not only expect some fine hospitality in the form of excellent food and drink, but also a warm and friendly welcome. Built in the early 1980s and so named to reflect the textile industry that played an important part in the area's history, the Flying Shuttle is managed by Karon and Frank Wallis.

As Frank is a master brewer no one will be surprised that the ales here are kept in tip top condition and there is always a guest ale on tap for connoisseurs to try. The food here too is delicious, with a bar menu served

The Flying Shuttle, Llanidloes Road, Newtown, Powys SY16 1HL
Tel: 01686 624688

during the week and, on Friday and Saturday evenings, a full, comprehensive list of home-cooked dishes is available. Visitors can choose to dine in the cosy, panelled rooms of the pub's interior or, weather permitting, in the attractive beer garden. The traditional Sunday lunches are always popular and, with the addition of a special children's menu, this is a great place to bring the whole family. However, this is not quite all the Flying Shuttle has to offer as on Saturday nights they lay on live entertainment and there is a disco each Friday evening.

At **Mochdre**, just to the south of Newtown, lies **Llettyderyn** a charming farmhouse, part of a small working sheep and beef rearing farm, that is reached up a long picturesque drive. The house, parts of which date back to the 18th century, was completely restored in the late 1980s, just before Margaret and John Jandrell moved here in 1990. From this attractive house,

Llettyderyn, Mochdre, near Newtown, Powys SY16 4JY
Tel: 01686 626131

the couple offer comfortable bed and breakfast accommodation in a choice of three en-suite guest rooms which, like the rest of the house are stylishly furnished and decorated. Though the house has been extensively modernised, many of the original features remain and, as well as the exposed beams and inglenook fireplace in the dining room, there is a traditional Welsh parlour, complete with a superb dresser.

Margaret's delicious home-cooked breakfast, with home-baked bread, sets everyone up for a day exploring the surrounding countryside and both packed lunches and more fantastic home-cooking at the evening meal are available. Ideal for children, there are not only panoramic views of the Dolfor Hills from the door step but also a middle distance farm walk that is well worth taking.

EAST OF NEWTOWN

LLANLLWCHAIARN   MAP 4 REF 18
2 miles NE of Newtown off the A483

Just through the village of Llanllwchaiarn, to the east of Newtown, lies **Lower Gwestydd**, an wonderful, attractive house that lies amid a sheep farm. This has been the home of Iris and David Jarman since the late 1970s and for most of their time here they have been offering excellent bed and breakfast accommodation from two en-suite rooms. The oldest part of the house dates back to the 11th century, but the main building

Lower Gwestydd, Llanllwchaiarn, near Newtown, Powys SY16 3AY
Tel: 01686 626718

was constructed in 1684 and it is of the typical black-and-white timber-framed style. To the front of the house is a charming, large well-tendered garden and also views over the nearby Kerry and Sarn Hills to the east.

As might be imagined with a house this age, there are lots of nooks and crannies and, only a few years ago, the couple unearthed a wonderful inglenook fireplace with a wooden bressumer which they have turned into an outstanding feature. However, guests at Lower Gwestydd will find that their every comfort is catered for and, once found, it is a hard place to leave.

ABER-MIWL   MAP 4 REF I8
4 miles NE of Newtown on B4386

Across the Montgomery Canal and River Severn from the village, which is also known by its English name **Abermule**, lie the few remains of **Dolforwyn Castle** which was built in 1273 by Llewelyn the Last. The last castle built by a native prince on his own soil, Llewellyn also tried to establish a small town around the castle to rival that of nearby and much anglicized Welshpool to the north. However, the castle was only a Welsh stronghold for four years before it was taken by the English and left to rot into the haunting ruins of today.

The **Abermule Hotel** is an impressive, black-and-white building that is hard to miss. In the heart of the village and opposite the railway line, the hotel was, in the 1920s, owned by a railway company and was, unimagi-

Abermule Hotel, Abermule, Powys SY15 6ND
Tel: 01686 630676

natively, called the Railway Hotel. As pretty as a picture in the summer with a mass of colourful hanging baskets and flower-filled window boxes, the Abermule Hotel is run by Adriana and Tegwyn Jerman. The couple maintain the hotel's tradition of offering hospitality to the traveller and this is certainly the place to come to for excellent food, drink, and accommodation.

Open all day, every day, there is a superb range of well kept ales behind the bar and the varied menu contains a list of delicious home-made specials. Accommodation is provided in a choice of three comfortable guest rooms that are let on a bed and breakfast basis or, for campers, there is a large field to the rear of the hotel, with four electric hook-ups, for caravans and tents. Children too are not forgotten and in the garden, at the back of the building, there is a wonderful, safe playarea with all manner of swings and climbing frames. Adults can also enjoy the country setting of the hotel by taking advantage of the outdoor seating.

MONTGOMERY   Map 4 ref J8
8 miles NE of Newtown on B4385

This attractive town, in its sheltered position, is well worth a visit. A market town with a pleasant Georgian character, there is also some attractive Tudor and Jacobean architecture. The local civic society has organised, to help the curious, a planned walk around the town which points out the places and buildings of interest.

Above the town the ruins of **Montgomery Castle** stand in affirmation of this area's turbulent history. Situated in part of the Marches, so called because this area was continually fought over and regarded as a 'wasteland', the castle played a part in this territorial struggle. Offa's Dyke passes close by and is another reminder of the military significance that this area once held. The castle, though, was first built around 1100 by the Norman, Roger de Montgomery. Stormed over the years by rebels, the castle was rebuilt in 1223 as a garrison as Henry III attempted to quell the Welsh, a consequence being that the town received a charter from the king in 1227. During the Civil War the castle was surrendered to Parliament forces but was demolished in 1649 in punishment for the then Lord Herbert's Royalist sympathies.

The 13th-century **St Nicholas' Church** has some interesting features but perhaps the most noteworthy is the Robber's Grave in the churchyard. John Davies, hanged in public in 1821 for murder, proclaimed his innocence and swore that the grass would not grow above his grave for at least 100 years!

To the west of the town the Iron Age hillfort **Fridd Faldwyn** tops a 750 foot hill which affords views over Cadair Idris and, eastwards, into England.

Situated in the heart of this historic town is **The Castle Kitchen**, a superb restaurant, tea rooms, and delicatessen that is housed in a charming 17th-century property. The brain child of proprietor David Willis, this excellent establishment is a must for anyone interested in fine food and top quality ingredients. The front of the premises is taken up with the excellent speciality shop that sells everything from loose tea and coffee beans, to aromatherapy oils and herbal remedies. Great care is taken in only selecting the very best goods for the shop and, with a wide range of organic foods, herbs and spices, local country preserves, and some superb Welsh, English, and Continental cheeses, there is certainly something to whet everyone's palate.

**The Castle Kitchen, Broad Street, Montgomery
Powys SY15 6PH Tel: 01686 668795**

To the rear and with a very cosy, olde worlde feel, is the characterful tea rooms where customers can sample some of the delicious fayre from the shop as well as enjoying a relaxing break. Beyond the tea rooms is a pretty garden and patio area that, as well as being secluded, is also a real sun trap. For more formal dining, the upstairs restaurant is the ideal choice. Open during the day, as is the shop and tea rooms, and in the evening on Friday and Saturday (also Thursdays in the summer), this excellent licensed restaurant again makes excellent use of the wonderful ingredients from the shop. This is certainly not a run-of-the-mill establishment and the reputation that The Castle Kitchen has gained is richly deserved.

CHURCH STOKE
10 miles E of Newtown on A489

MAP 4 REF J8

This attractive village lies right on the Welsh-English border and, just to the west, can be found some very visible and well preserved sections of Offa's Dyke.

The Horse and Jockey is a quaint old pub, dating back some 250 years, found in the heart of Welsh border country. This charming inn has been owned and personally run by Kay and Paul Digby since 1995 and, as well as being extremely hospitable hosts, Paul is also a chef by trade. Not surprisingly, the food here comes highly recommended by locals and visitors alike and the interesting menu alone makes a visit here very worthwhile. The restaurant area, like the rest of the pub, is very cosy and intimate with the building's original ceiling beams and exposed thick stone walls very much in evidence. The olde worlde atmosphere is enhanced by the display of memorabilia on the walls.

The Horse and Jockey, Church Stoke, Powys SY15 6AE
Tel: 01588 620060

The bar area, where a range of excellent real ales are served, not only features a large and welcoming fire but also a traditional quarry tiled floor. Open every day, except non-Bank Holiday Mondays, the Horse and Jockey is a superb place to visit for the whole family. To the rear of the premises, behind the much used beer garden, is a well-maintained caravan park with 20 hard standing pitches complete with electric hook-ups and an ablution block.

KERRY
3 miles E of Newtown on A489

MAP 4 REF 18

On the banks of the River Mule, a tributary of the River Severn, this village is famous for its beautiful 12th-century Church of St Michael and All Angels. To the south, taking in Kerry Hill and Ceri Forest, is the relatively short but pleasant Kerry Ridgeway Footpath which begins close to the source of the River Ithon and travels eastwards, across the border, to Bishop's Castle.

In the heart of the village lies **The Kerry Lamb Inn**, a charming village pub which dates from the 18th century, though it was extended in the 19th century and became known as The New Inn. Changing its name back to The Kerry Lamb in the 1970s, the inn, which is open all day until

The Kerry Lamb Inn, Kerry, near Newtown, Powys SY16 4NP
Tel: 01686 670226

15.00, every day except Tuesday, in the summer is a charming place run by excellent hosts Rhian and Derrick Davies. One of the great features of the pub is the Kerry Lamb ale, brewed for the inn and, whilst this is certainly worth tasting, there are many other draught ales and lagers on tap.

Much of the inn's new found popularity, however, stems from the delicious food that is served at both lunchtime and in the evening. This is Rhian's department and, as well as the more usual dishes, the varied menu and the weekend specials' board has a number of more interesting dishes: the traditional Sunday roast lunch is also always popular. The cosy and comfortable interior compliments perfectly the striking exterior, with its cream painted walls and colourful, flower-filled hanging baskets.

WEST OF NEWTOWN

CAERSWS   MAP 4 REF I8
4 miles W of Newtown off A470

The village is built on the site of a 1st-century Roman fort that was strategically positioned here by the Rivers Severn and Carno and, to the north
of Caersws, the earthworks of the fort can still be seen. In more recent
times, Caersws was the home, for 20 years, of the poet John 'Ceiriog'
Hughes.

LLANDINAM   MAP 4 REF H9
6 miles W of Newtown on A470

This quiet village was once the home of David Davies, an industrialist who
was instrumental in founding the docks at Barry, in south Wales. Davies'
bronze statue, made by Sir Alfred Gilbert who was also responsible for Eros
in Piccadilly, lies in the village.

LLANIDLOES   MAP 4 REF H9
10 miles W of Newtown on A470

This peaceful, small market town is certainly one of the area's prettiest and
its adaptability, from a rural village to a weaving town and, now, to a
centre for craftspeople, has ensured that it is likely to remain so for years
to come. John Wesley preached here three times in the mid 1700s and the
stone from which he addressed his audience stands outside the **Museum
of Local History and Industry**. Inside are displays and information on
textile and mining industries that were rife in the area during the 18th
and 19th centuries. In 1839, the town was a focal point of the bitter
Chartist Riots after the Reform Bill of 1832 had failed to meet demands
that included universal suffrage and social equality. The museum is housed
in the **Old Market Hall** which is a wonderful half-timbered building from
around 1600. The upper floor was originally a court house and was later
used by Quakers, Baptists and Methodists as a meeting place.

To the northwest lies **Llyn Clywedog**, a reservoir developed in the mid
1960s to regulate the flows of the Rivers Severn and Clywedog. Roads
follow around both sides of the lake, with the B4518 curving round the
slopes of the 1,580 feet of Tan Hill, where the disused **Van Lead Mine** and
surrounding deserted houses of a once thriving town and industry can be
visited.

The Red Lion, on Llanidloes' main street, is hard to miss as this former
18th-century coaching inn is a beautifully preserved building that is as
attractive now as it was in the heyday of coach travel. Not surprisingly,

**The Red Lion, 8 Longbridge Street, Llanidloes, Powys SY18 6EE
Tel: 01686 412270 Fax: 01686 413120**

this charming black and white painted building is also listed and, equally surprisingly, the interior matches up to the expectations of the exterior. Managed by David Taylor, this wonderful old inn is a carefully blended mix of the cosy charm of yesteryear and the top class attention and hospitality expected by today's modern traveller. The bar, always a popular place, serves a good range of real ales, including Hancocks HB and Bass, in the very traditional atmosphere created by the beamed ceiling and the inglenook fireplace.

The food here too is certainly not the normal pub food, although customers wanting a sandwich will not be disappointed with the mouth-watering choice available. However, the menu in the separate dining room, which is open at both lunchtimes and in the evening, is interesting and imaginative, blending ingredients from near and far with the best of Welsh produce. However, this is not all, as The Red Lion also boasts 10 superior en-suite guest rooms, three of which are self-catering flats.

Dating back to 1896, **The Coach and Horses** in the heart of Llanidloes is a charming former coaching inn, with its original stable block still standing, that is owned and personally run by Chris and Tony Cox. Well known for its fine selection of real ales available from the bar and delicious bar snacks, this is a warm and friendly pub that proves popular with local and visiting families alike. As well as the excellent hospitality, there is a comfortable lounge bar, decorated with pictures of submarines, reflecting Tony's past life in the navy, and large cats - a keen interest of Chris's. There is also

**The Coach and Horses, 12 Smithfield Street, Llanidloes
Powys SY18 6EJ Tel: 01686 412266**

a children's room, a games room upstairs, and, outside, a delightful beer garden with an aviary. Entertainment, in the form of live music, is put on most weekends and the pub is open all day, every day except Tuesdays when The Coach and Horses opens for the evening only. Finally, Chris and Tony also offer superb bed and breakfast accommodation, all year round, in a choice of three comfortable and cosy guest rooms. Those staying overnight, however, should look out for the friendly pub ghost!

Situated just outside the village of **Trefeglwys**, to the north of Llanidloes, and close to the beautiful Clywedog Reservoir, **Cefngwyn** lies in the heart of some superb countryside. This mixed farm, like the attractive farmhouse, is owned by Joan and Cyril Williams and they have, for nearly 30 years, been offering some of the best bed and breakfast accommodation to be found, anywhere. The first sight guests have of this ideal holiday destination is the delightful garden surrounding the house, well laid out and carefully tended which sets the tone for guests' relaxing stay. There are three excellent guest rooms which, as well as being en-suite, have been thoughtfully decorated and furnished with comfort and style high on the list of priorities. Guests too can enjoy outstanding views, from the bedrooms as well as the sitting room and dining room, over the rolling mid Wales countryside that is uninterrupted in every direction. Delicious farmhouse cooking is also a key aspect of any stay at Cefngwyn and home-made

Cefngwyn, Trefeglwys, near Caersws, Powys SY17 5RF
Tel: 01686 430648

cakes are the house speciality. All in all, Cefngwyn is a treat not to be missed.

MACHYNLLETH

Pronounced Mah-hun-cthleth, this small town is a popular, but not over-crowded, holiday centre. It was here that Owain Glyndwr held his first parliament in 1404 and a part 15th-century building stands on the site which is home to the **Owain Glyndwr Centre**. Apart from the displays telling the life story of Glyndwr, through his military campaigns to the

Owain Glyndwr Centre, Machynlleth

time of his downfall, there are details of the parliament held in Machynlleth, from where Glyndwr controlled most of Wales as it is recognised today. Opposite the centre is the entrance to **Plas Machynlleth**, an elegenat mansion built in 1653, which was given to the town by Lord Londonderry and is now used as council offices; its grounds are, however, a public area.

At the centre of the town is an ornate **Clock Tower**; dating from 1872; it was built by public subscription to mark the coming of age of Lord Castlereagh, heir to the Marquess of Londonderry. From the tower, Maengwyn Street, the town's broad main street, runs eastwards. As well as being home to the Owain Glyndwr Centre and Plas Machynlleth, on the south side of street stands the so-called **Mayor's House**, a half-timbered building dating from 1628 and also the **Welsh Museum of Modern Art**, which offers not only permanent collections but many touring exhibitions.

Conveniently situated on the main street, **The Rendezvous Café** is the ideal place to stop and enjoy a quiet sit down and some real home-cooking. Although Daphne and John Wright, the café's owners have only been here since April 1998, they have many years experience in the catering trade and this is put to excellent use in providing customers with the perfect haven from a busy day's shopping. Open all day, every day except Sundays, the menu and specials board list a mouth-watering array of dishes that include all the favourites and more besides. Wednesday is market day in Machynlleth and the special roast lunches served here between noon and 14.30 are well worth trying. Cosy and comfortably furnished, with a separate non-smoking area, the café also offers its customers the chance to relax and take a breather at any time of day.

The Rendezvous Café, Maengwyn Street, Machynlleth, Powys SY20 8EB Tel: 01654 702326

EAST OF MACHYNLLETH

PENEGOES
MAP 3 REF G8
2 miles E of Machynlleth on A489

For an interesting and unusual day out, the **Centre for Alternative Technology**, founded in 1975, is an excellent place for all the family. Europe's leading eco-centre, there are displays and exhibits illustrating the various sources of energy available as well as an organic garden, an adventure playground, and a vegetarian restaurant.

LLAN
MAP 3 REF H8
9 miles E of Machynlleth on B4518

Found on the banks of the River Twymyn, this hamlet was the birthplace of Abraham Rees who published an edition of *Ephraim Chambers Cyclopedia* between 1778-88 having added something like 4500 new pieces of information. Llan was also home of the social reformer, Reverend Samuel Roberts, who advocated social equality and temperance, and was instrumental in the reform of postal services.

DYLIFE
MAP 3 REF H8
8 miles E of Machynlleth off B4518

Apart from an inn and a few houses, there is little is left of this once prosperous lead mining community. The footpath from the settlement passes close to the grassy mound that was once a Roman fort, built here, it is believed, to guard the nearby lead mines. The path continues past more redundant lead mines that were last worked during the late 17th century before it meanders through a woodland, following the banks of River Clywedog, and towards the Staylittle. The final part of the route lies close to a Bronze Age tumuli that suggests that mining occurred in the area even before the Roman occupation. Close by Staylittle, a one-time lead mining village, is said to have derived its name from the two blacksmiths who shoed horses so rapidly that their forge became known as Stay-a-Little. In a remote area high in the Cambrian Mountains, Staylittle is on the edge of the Hafren Forest and Llyn Clywedog.

WEST OF MACHYNLLETH

EGLWYS-FACH
MAP 3 REF F8
5 miles W of Machynlleth on A487

Also known as **Furnace**, this was a place of silver refining and iron smelting. **Dyfi Furnace**, dating from the 18th century, is an industrial heritage site and museum that has a fully operational waterwheel. This site was first used in the 17th century to refine silver by using the waterpower of the River Einion, later it was used as a charcoal burning blast furnace for iron.

The road opposite the site leads up the Cwm Einion which is sometimes called the Artists' Valley as it was popular with 19th-century watercolourists. Woodland trails and picnic spots combine to make this a lovely area to visit and spend the day. **Dyfi National Reserve**, where access is restricted because of dangerous tidal waters, is a corner of the Dyfi estuary that is used by many waders and wildfowl.

Found halfway between Aberystwyth and Machynlleth, at **Tre'r-ddôl** just south of Eglwys-fach, **The Wildfowler Inn** is a charming early 18th-century public house that is owned and personally run by Lynn and Gary with the help of brother Mark and sister Delyth. Inn-keeping must run in the family as mother and father, Sylvia and Ron, run the Black Lion at nearby Talybont. Known as the Commercial Hotel for many years, the inn was renamed to reflect the birdlife of the area which is famous for the ducks that live on the Dyfi estuary close by.

The inn too has much to offer both visitors and locals alike. As well as the excellent range of real ales, this characterful place has a fine reputation for the high standard of the delicious home-cooked meals that are served here everyday. The comprehensive menu, supplemented by a list of daily specials, makes the very best of the freshest local ingredients and, as well as featuring duck, there is also a good selection of fish, meat, and vegetarian dishes from which to choose. Well known and popular locally, it is always advisable to book a table in the restaurant to avoid disappointment. However, this is not all that The Wildfowler has to offer as there are

The Wildfowler Inn, Tre'r-ddôl, Machynlleth, Powys SY20 8PN
Tel: 01970 832671

three comfortable en-suite guest rooms that, as well as providing all the usual amenities, are as stylishly decorated and as full of character as the rest of the inn.

BORTH   MAP 3 REF F8
11 miles SW of Machynlleth on B4353

A popular seaside resort half way along the Cardigan Bay coast, Borth is surrounded by fine scenery. The original settlement was located on the slopes of Rhiw Fawr, Upper Borth, and some of the older fishermen's and farmers' cottages remain. The growth of the village as a resort really took off in 1863 with the coming of the Aberystwyth and Welsh Coast Railway. The path, leading from the village's War Memorial, provides an exhilarating walk along the cliff tops to Clarach and Aberystwyth.

TOURIST
INFORMATION
CENTRES

Centres in **bold** are open all the year around.

Aberdyfi Tourist Information Centre
   The Wharf Gardens, Aberdyfi, LL35 0ED
   Tel No: 01654 767321

Bala Tourist Information Centre
   Penllyn, Pensran Road, Bala, LL23 7SR
   Tel & Fax No: 01678 521021

Bangor Tourist Information Centre
   Little Chef Services, A55/A5, Bangor, LL57 7BG
   Tel No: 01248 352786

Barmouth Tourist Information Centre
   The Old Library, Station Road, Barmouth, LL42 1LU
   Tel No: 01341 280787

Betws-Y-Coed Tourist Information Centre
   Royal Oaks Stables, Betws-Y-Coed, LL42 0AH
   Tel No: 01690 710426 Fax No: 01690 710665

Blaenau Ffestiniog Tourist Information Centre
   Isallt, High Street, Blaenau Ffestiniog, LL41 3HD
   Tel No: 01766 830360

Borth Tourist Information Centre
High Street, The Promenade, Borth, SY24 5HY
Tel No: 01970 871174

Caernarfon Tourist Information Centre
Oriel Pendetish, Castel Street, Caernarfon, LL55 2NA
Tel No: 01286 672232

Colwyn Bay Tourist Information Centre
40 Station Bay, Colwyn Bay, LL29 8BU
Tel No: 01492 530478 Fax No: 01492 530789

Conwy Tourist Information Centre
Conwy Castle Visitors Centre, Conwy, LL32 8LD
Tel No: 01492 592248

Corris Tourist Information Centre
Corris Craft Centre, Nr Machynlleth, Corris, SY20 9SP
Tel No: 01654 761224

Dolgellau Tourist Information Centre
Ty Meirion, Eldon Square, Dolgellau, LL40 1PU
Tel & Fax No: 01341 422888

Ewloe Tourist Information Centre
Autolodge Site, Gateway Services - A55 West, Ewloe, CH7 6HE
Tel No: 01244 541597

Harlech Tourist Information Centre
Gwyddfor House, High Street, Harlech, LL46 2YA
Tel No: 01766 780658

Holyhead Tourist Information Centre
Marine Square, Salt Island Approach, Holyhead, LL65 1DR
Tel No: 01407 762622

Lake Vrynwy Tourist Information Centre
Unit 2, Vrynwy Craft Workshops, Lake Vrynwy, SY10 0LY
Tel No: 01691 870346

Llanberis Tourist Information Centre
41B High Street, Llanberis, LL55 4EH
Tel No: 01286 870765

Llandudno Tourist Information Centre
1-2 Chapel Street, Llandudno, LL30 2YU
Tel No: 01492 876413 Fax No: 01492 872722

Llanfair PG Tourist Information Centre
Station Site, Isle Of Anglessy, Llanfair, LL61 5UJ
Tel No: 01248 713177

Llangollen Tourist Information Centre
Town Hall, Castle Street, Llangollen, LL20 5PD
Tel No: 01978 860828

Llanidloes Tourist Information Centre
Longbridge Street, Llanidloes, SY18 6BN
Tel No: 01686 412605

Machynlleth Tourist Information Centre
Canclfan Owain Glyndwr, Machynlleth, SY20 8EE
Tel No: 01654 702401 Fax No: 01654 703675

Mold Tourist Information Centre
Library, Museum, Earl Road, Mold, CH7 1AP
Tel No: 01352 759331

Newtown Tourist Information Centre
Central Car Park, Newtown, SY16 2PW
Tel No: 01686 625580

Porthmadog Tourist Information Centre
High Street, Porthmadog, LL49 9LP
Tel No: 01766 512981

Prestatyn Tourist Information Centre
Scala Cinema, High Street, Prestatyn, LL19 9LH
Tel No: 01745 889092

Pwllheli Tourist Information Centre
Min-Y-Don, Station Road, Pwllheli, LL53 6HE
Tel No: 01758 613000

Rhos-On-Sea Tourist Information Centre
The Promenade, Rhos-On-Sea, LL28 4EP
Tel No: 01492 548778

Rhyl Tourist Information Centre
Rhyl Childrens Village, West Parade, Rhyl, LL18 1HZ
Tel No: 01745 355068

Ruthin Tourist Information Centre
Ruthin Craft Centre, Park Road, Ruthin, LL15 1BB
Tel No: 01824 703992

Tywyn Tourist Information Centre
High Street, Tywyn, LL36 9AD
Tel No: 01654 710070

Welshpool Tourist Information Centre
Flash Centre, Salop Road, Welshpool, SY21 7DH
Tel No: 01938 552043

Wrexham Tourist Information Centre
Lambpit Street, Wrexham, LL11 1AY
Tel No: 01978 292015 Fax No: 01978 290091

INDEX OF TOWNS, VILLAGES AND PLACES OF INTEREST

INDEX OF PLACES TO STAY, EAT, DRINK & SHOP

Chapter 2: South Snowdonia

Chapter 5: Vale of Clwyd and East Conwy

Chapter 6: Gateway to Wales

Chapter 7: Llangollen and the Ruabon Mountains

Chapter 8: North Powys

Chapter 9: Mid Powys

ACCOMMODATION

Abermule Hotel	Abermule	207	4I8
Cefngwyn	Trefeglwys	214	4H9
Coach and Horses	Llanidloes	213	4H9
Horse and Jockey	Church Stoke	210	4J8
Llettyderyn	Mochdre	205	4I8
Lower Gwestydd	Llanllwchaiarn	206	4I8
Pheasant Inn	Newtown	203	4I8
Red Lion	Llanidloes	212	4H9
Wildfowler Inn	Nr Machynlleth	218	3F8

PUBS, INNS AND WINEBARS

Abermule Hotel	Abermule	207	4I8
Coach and Horses	Llanidloes	213	4H9
Flying Shuttle	Newtown	204	4I8
Horse and Jockey	Church Stoke	210	4J8
Kerry Lamb Inn	Kerry	211	4I8
Pheasant Inn	Newtown	203	4I8
Red Lion	Llanidloes	212	4H9
Wildfowler Inn	Nr Machynlleth	218	3F8

RESTAURANTS

Castle Kitchen	Montgomery	209	4J8
Jays Restaurant	Newtown	203	4I8
Red Lion	Llanidloes	212	4H9
Wildfowler Inn	Nr Machynlleth	218	3F8

TEA ROOMS, COFFEE SHOPS & CAFÉS

Castle Kitchen	Montgomery	209	4J8
Rendezvous Café	Machynlleth	216	3G8

THE HIDDEN PLACES
Order Form

To order any of our publications just fill in the payment details below and complete the order form *overleaf*. For orders of less than 4 copies please add £1 per book for postage and packing. Orders over 4 copies are P & P free.

Please Complete Either:

I enclose a cheque for £ .... made payable to Travel Publishing Ltd

Or:

Card No: ☐☐☐☐ ☐☐☐☐ ☐☐☐☐ ☐☐☐☐

Expiry Date: ☐☐ ☐☐

Signature: ....

NAME: ....

ADDRESS: ....

....

....

POSTCODE: ....

TEL NO: ....

Please send to: Travel Publishing Ltd
7a Apollo House
Calleva Park
Aldermaston
Berks, RG7 8TN

THE HIDDEN PLACES
Order Form

	Price	Quantity	Value
Regional Titles			
Cambridgeshire & Lincolnshire	£7.99	....	....
Channel Islands	£6.99	....	....
Cheshire	£7.99	....	....
Cornwall	£7.99	....	....
Devon	£7.99	....	....
Dorset, Hants & Isle of Wight	£4.95	....	....
Essex	£7.99	....	....
Gloucestershire	£6.99	....	....
Heart of England	£4.95	....	....
Highlands & Islands	£7.99	....	....
Kent	£7.99	....	....
Lake District & Cumbria	£7.99	....	....
Lancashire	£7.99	....	....
Norfolk	£7.99	....	....
Northeast Yorkshire	£6.99	....	....
Northumberland & Durham	£6.99	....	....
North Wales	£7.99	....	....
Nottinghamshire	£6.99	....	....
Peak District	£6.99	....	....
Potteries	£6.99	....	....
Somerset	£6.99	....	....
South Wales	£4.95	....	....
Suffolk	£7.99	....	....
Surrey	£6.99	....	....
Sussex	£6.99	....	....
Thames & Chilterns	£5.99	....	....
Warwickshire & West Midlands	£7.99	....	....
Welsh Borders	£5.99	....	....
Wiltshire	£6.99	....	....
Yorkshire Dales	£6.99	....	....
Set of any 5 Regional titles	**£25.00**	....	....
National Titles			
England	£9.99	....	....
Ireland	£8.99	....	....
Scotland	£8.99	....	....
Wales	£8.99	....	....
Set of all 4 National titles	**£28.00**	....	....
		_____	_____
		_____	_____

For orders of less than 4 copies please add £1 per book for postage & packing. Orders over 4 copies P & P free.

THE HIDDEN PLACES
───── Reader Comment Form ─────

The *Hidden Places* research team would like to receive reader's comments on any visitor attractions or places reviewed in the book and also recommendations for suitable entries to be included in the next edition. This will help ensure that the *Hidden Places* series continues to provide its readers with useful information on the more interesting, unusual or unique features of each attraction or place ensuring that their stay in the local area is an enjoyable and stimulating experience.

To provide your comments or recommendations would you please complete the forms below and overleaf as indicated and send to: The Research Department, Travel Publishing Ltd., 7a Apollo House, Calleva Park, Aldermaston, Reading, RG7 8TN.

Your Name:

Your Address:

Your Telephone Number:

Please tick as appropriate: Comments ☐   Recommendation ☐

Name of *"Hidden Place"*:

Address:

Telephone Number:

Name of Contact:

THE HIDDEN PLACES
──── Reader Comment Form ────

Comment or Reason for Recommendation:

....

....

....

....

....

....

....

....

....

....

....

....

THE HIDDEN PLACES
——— Reader Comment Form ———

The *Hidden Places* research team would like to receive reader's comments on any visitor attractions or places reviewed in the book and also recommendations for suitable entries to be included in the next edition. This will help ensure that the *Hidden Places* series continues to provide its readers with useful information on the more interesting, unusual or unique features of each attraction or place ensuring that their stay in the local area is an enjoyable and stimulating experience.

To provide your comments or recommendations would you please complete the forms below and overleaf as indicated and send to: The Research Department, Travel Publishing Ltd., 7a Apollo House, Calleva Park, Aldermaston, Reading, RG7 8TN.

Your Name:

Your Address:

Your Telephone Number:

Please tick as appropriate: Comments ☐   Recommendation ☐

Name of *"Hidden Place"*:

Address:

Telephone Number:

Name of Contact:

THE HIDDEN PLACES
—— Reader Comment Form ——

Comment or Reason for Recommendation:

....

....

....

....

....

....

....

....

....

....

....

....

MAP SECTION

The following pages of maps encompass the main cities, towns and geographical features of North Wales, as well as many of the interesting places featured in the guide. Distances are indicated by the use of scale bars located below each of the maps

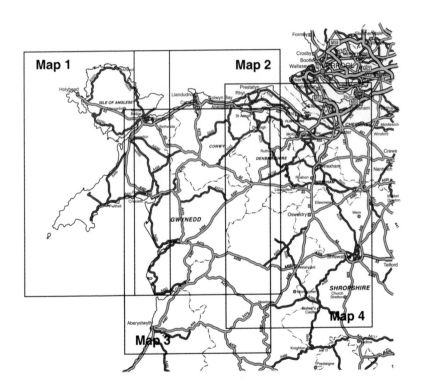

© MAPS IN MINUTES ™ (1998)

MAP 1

© MAPS IN MINUTES ™ (1998)

MAP 2

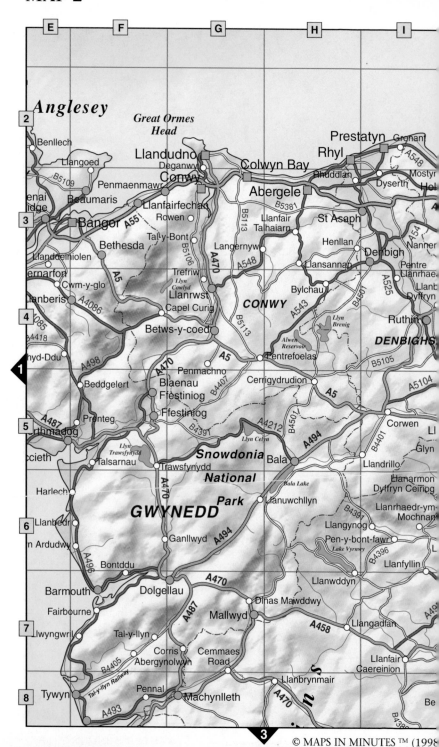

© MAPS IN MINUTES ™ (1998

MAP 3

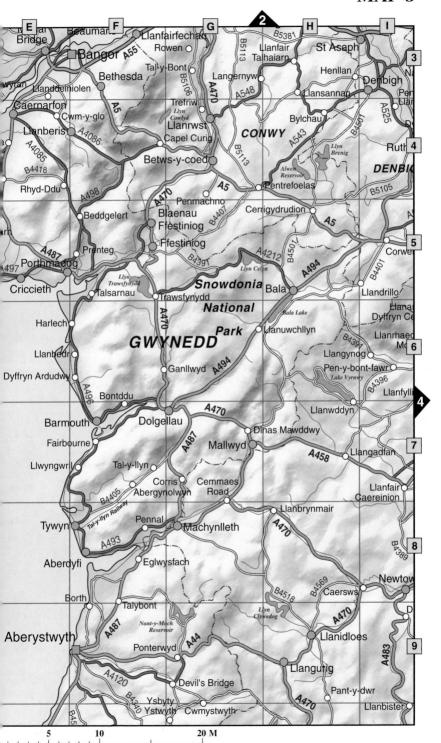

5 10 20 M

MAP 4

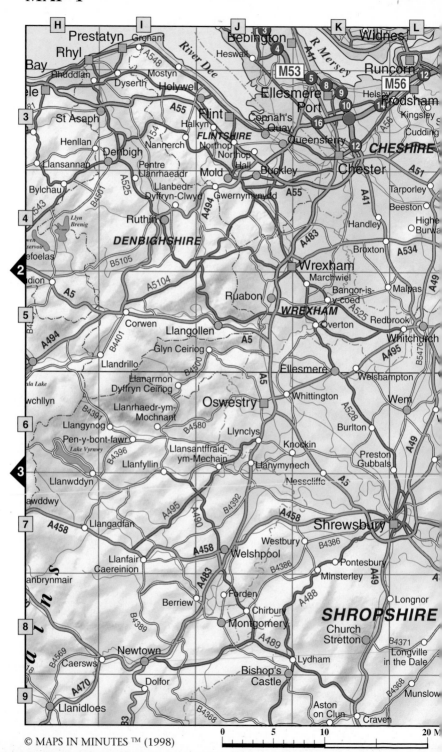

0   5   10   20 M